HOW UNEXPECTED
HONESTY AND
UNDERSTANDING
THE BUYING BRAIN
CAN TRANSFORM
YOUR RESULTS

The Transparency Sale

TODD CAPONI

IDEAPRESS
PUBLISHING

WASHINGTON, DC

IDEAPRESS
PUBLISHING

Originally published in hardcover in 2018 by Ideapress Publishing.

Published in the United States by Ideapress Publishing.

Ideapress Publishing | www.ideapresspublishing.com

All trademarks are the property of their respective companies.

Cover Design by FACEOUT STUDIOS

Cataloging-in-Publication Data is on file with the Library of Congress.

ISBN: 978-1-64687-0226

Proudly Printed in the United States of America

Special Sales

Ideapress Books are available at a special discount for bulk purchases
for sales promotions and premiums, or for use in corporate training
programs. Special editions, including personalized covers, a custom
foreword, corporate imprints and bonus content are also available.

To my mother-in-law, Sandy, who,
with all she was dealing with in the final years of her life,
always encouraged me to write ...and was my biggest fan.

TABLE OF CONTENTS

SECTION 5: WHY STAY, BUY MORE & ADVOCATE?

BONUS CHAPTER

INTRODUCTION

O N A LAZY SATURDAY MORNING IN MARCH OF 2017, MY SIX-YEAR-old daughter and I were sitting in our family room. With her child-proof padded iPad perched on her lap, my daughter spoke, "Princess games," into the App Store search bar using the voice-to-text function. Sitting across from her on our L-shaped couch, I was scrolling through family-friendly movie options on Netflix.

In one thirty-second interval, my daughter selected an app to download, and then looked up at the TV screen. Without hesitation, she helped me decide whether a movie option was worthy of her Saturday morning. She had not heard of any of the games she was scrolling through on her iPad before making her decision. She hadn't yet mastered reading. We had not even heard of the majority of the movie options we were scrolling through on Netflix. How did she decide on a game with such confidence, without even being able to read the descriptions?

"That app has 4 stars, which is better than these 2 and 3 star ones. And that movie has a cute bunny, and almost 5 stars."

Given that I had spent nearly four years building one of Chicago's fastest growing technology companies, PowerReviews, I have often wondered whether I had created a review-dependent monster out of her. Reviews were in my blood... and perhaps hers, too.

Looking at the world right now, it's clear that this isn't limited to my family of course. It's everyone...young and old, male and female. Today, children (aka "our future buyers") are growing up surrounded by reviews and feedback on everything they interact with. Adults are becoming dependent on them as well. These present and future buyers have an expectation of transparency, where their decisions are influenced by user-submitted feedback listed right alongside the options they are deciding upon. In some cases, we have even become incapable of making a selection without the aid of these reviews.

We, as consumers, are quickly becoming reliant on picking restaurants, hotels, products, and experiences based on reviews and star ratings shared online more than ever before. We are even rating our services, like Uber drivers. And those Uber drivers are rating us back. Perhaps even more concerning for anyone in business is that consumers often trust those reviews more than they trust what the organizations providing those products and services say.

When my daughter chose the movie she wanted to watch, she wasn't choosing based on movie posters or meticulously scripted and edited trailers. The rating was the only thing that mattered.

It's easy to think that this is just an extreme example. Marketing has to play a part, doesn't it? What about the importance of the salesperson?

I have spent nearly all of my career working in sales and everything I learned was about the importance of the relationship. There are countless books on how to close deals, build your network, be a trusted advisor, and nurture relationships. So I couldn't help thinking, surely sales, which has always been highly dependent on personal relationships, could never be reduced to mere reviews? This question drove me to spend the next year exploring the shifting evolution of how to sell effectively in a world filled with on-demand reviews. It led me to uncover one startling truth that drove me to write this book.

To understand this truth, we should start with a quick review of some interesting research into how consumers research and buy the things they need online today. According to research:

- 95% of consumers use reviews for their online purchases, with 86% considering them to be an important part of their purchase journey.[1]
- 82% of consumers specifically seek out negative reviews when making a purchase.[2]
- Purchase likelihood peaks when the average star rating of a product is between 4.2 and 4.5 stars (on a 5 star scale).[3]

Let's consider that again.

A product with a 4.2 star rating sells better than one with a perfect 5.0. Inherently this makes sense. Our brains are wired to resist being "sold-to" and so this is an understandable defense mechanism.

It also leads to the single truth at the heart of this book:

TRANSPARENCY SELLS BETTER THAN PERFECTION.

We have been taught to sell perfection, but perfection does not sell. To win in this digital era, where feedback is all around us and easy to come by, we need to adjust how we sell to optimize for the way buyers buy.

The Transparency Sale is about giving people all of the information the brain requires to feel confident about making a decision. It's about framing our solutions as a 4.2-4.5, and no longer positioning as though we're a perfect 5.0. It's about understanding how feelings and emotions influence the decisions buyers

---

1   PowerReviews (2014): The Proven Power of Reviews.

2   PowerReviews (2014): The Proven Power of Reviews.

3   From Reviews to Revenue, PowerReviews, 2015, spiegel.medill.northwestern.edu/_pdf/Online%20Reviews%20Whitepaper.pdf

make. It's about how your potential prospects and buyers make the majority of their decisions subconsciously, understanding that the selling cycle isn't just about getting your buyers to make one decision...to buy from you. The selling cycle requires a recognition that the buyer is making hundreds or even thousands of subconscious micro-decisions.

How would I make leading with unexpected honesty, sharing vulnerabilities, and optimizing every interaction based on how the brain engages and makes decisions work? I began to mess around with the concept of how to talk about our products' shortcomings with buyers, and sharing the fact that some buyers found our competitors' offerings more appealing.

In my own experience, the use of unexpected honesty and transparency shortened sales cycles dramatically. In one instance, what was normally a six-month sales cycle closed in our favor in under a month. In another, the head of e-commerce for a major fashion brand kicked his team out of the office, grabbed a folder filled with spreadsheets containing his fiscal budget, and walked me through it line-by-line. Before these experiments, I had never encountered a buyer (a term I use loosely to describe anyone who is being influenced) who was willing to show me their actual budget, much less during the first meeting. After employing this technique, one buyer actually sold ME on why the competitive offering I had presented as a differentiator in the competitor's favor wasn't valuable at all, and why we were correct in our choice not to develop that same functionality.

Through this approach, I found that the relationship between our sellers (a term I use loosely to describe anyone who is influencing a potential buyer) and their buyers was situating on a rock-solid foundation of trust. Sellers spent less time on opportunities they should have disqualified as being worthy of their time investment from the beginning. Buyers became less likely to believe any false claims that a competitor made because trust and openness was established from the first conversation. And, when something went wrong once the buyer was a customer, addressing those issues became incredibly easy, as expectations were set properly pre-sale.

Prior to the digital age we're all living in, salespeople had the power. Buyers *needed* sellers. Buyers had limited means to research your products, your services, and your pricing without actually communicating with you, the seller. There were a limited number of options for getting questions answered, so buyers often *wanted* to communicate with you. Believe it or not, there was a time when buyers consistently picked up their phone when you called. A mistruth or flaw about a product or service could not be shared consumer-to-consumer in an easy way. Up until the 1990s, the only way to complain about a product was to pick up the phone and call the company the purchase was made from... or even less effective, write a letter.

Today, by the time you actually get to talk to a buyer (one study states that it now takes eighteen dials on average to connect with a prospect[4]), they have likely self-diagnosed their own pain, researched potential solutions, have formed opinions on the potential solutions available to them, and are armed with data to support their opinions...data which they didn't get from you.

Today's digital era has brought with it rapid advancements in technology, information accessibility, and our understanding of how the brain makes decisions. Ironically, this technology has also shifted all of the power to the buyers. When you attempt to reach out to those buyers, they're using technology like caller ID on their phones to avoid you, email to avoid speaking to you, and voice mail systems that now are able to transcribe your words to text so they don't even have to hear your voice!

It's time to regain the power back.

---

4   "Sales Development Technology: The Stack Emerges." TOPO Blog, 22 May 2015, blog. topohq.com/sales-development-technology-the-stack-emerges/

This starts with a better understanding of our buying brain: the way that we make decisions as consumers. Beyond reviews or striving for authenticity, building a better understanding of how decision making really works is key to getting better at selling anything to anyone. In this book, we will take the latest insights from decision science and merge them with a broader understanding of consumer influence. Ultimately, this blend will help you to make your own Transparency Sale when it really matters.

In particular, the book will cover the following topics:

SECTION 1: TRANSPARENCY REDEFINED

Considering our requirement as sales professionals to ease the path for buyers to make the countless decisions required throughout the sales process, these first four chapters are written to teach you the fundamentals of *The Transparency Sale*. We'll explore the fundamental truths of how the brain makes decisions (Chapter 1), how every interaction with a potential buyer is either building or eroding trust (Chapter 2), the Results Formula which will be used to measure the impact of changes you make (Chapter 3), and finally basing your sales process on the recognition of where a buyer is in their journey (Chapter 4).

SECTION 2: WHY CHANGE?

In your efforts to drive buyers to decide to change from what they're doing today to something new, we will apply the concepts from Section 1 to prospecting with a special focus on digital communication (Chapter 5), positioning your products and services with unexpected honesty (Chapter 6), and the power of Mutual Decision Plans (Chapter 7).

SECTION 3: WHY YOU?

Once the buyer is shaken from their status quo and recognizes the need to change, the conversation usually shifts to why they should make that change with you. In Chapter 8, we'll build a presentation choreography that not only tells a great story, but also both compels the listener to action, and through the use of brain science, quickly brings a group together in their thinking. In Chapter 9, we'll also briefly explore the use of references in your sales cycles, both in how to empower the references and how to shift the way in which you approach and build references for your products.

SECTION 4: WHY NOW?

Building trust does not need to end once your buyer has selected you and your company. Negotiation and contract finalization no longer need to be about starting at opposite ends of the table, and hoping to end up in the middle. In Chapter 10, I'll teach you the concept of Transparent Negotiations, and in Chapter 11, we'll explore ways to maintain momentum in your sales cycles through the contract Ts & Cs (Terms & Conditions) process.

SECTION 5: WHY STAY, BUY MORE & ADVOCATE?

Sales doesn't stop when the contract is signed. There is no easier path to more sales than through current customers, relationships, and rock-solid trust. In Section 5, we will briefly discuss the vitally important moments following signature through your Post-Purchase Interaction (Chapter 12). And, in Chapter 13, we'll apply the concepts of *The Transparency Sale* to the world of Client Success.

Finally, we'll end with a "Bonus Chapter" (Chapter 14), which explores the application of these concepts to your next job search, to your recruiting efforts, to managing a team, and a different way to think about maximizing your investment at conferences in how you set up your booth.

As the former Chairman and CEO of GE, Jack Welch was quoted as saying, "Change before you have to." The use of unexpected honesty and transparency is still rare. Transparency wins, and now there is science to back it up...science, which can be applied to every element of your sales arsenal. There is an advantage waiting for you inside the pages of this book.

Then, it is my hope you will leave a review wherever you picked up the book, and that the score will average out to a solid 4.5!

SECTION 1:

TRANSPARENCY REDEFINED

suggestions to change course. The brain's neocortex (governing thought and logic) takes more energy to function than any other portion of the brain. In making a change, as we sales professionals are calling on the neocortex to justify a purchase, it takes the brain more effort to think about and do something new than it does to act instinctively or out of habit.[1]

In a University College London study, it was found that the amount of effort an individual *perceives* in doing anything actually changes what our brains see.[2] Anything challenging is perceived in our brains to be a less attractive option. If we haven't painted a picture of an easy path to evaluate, purchase, implement, and use our products, that uncertainty may drive a buyer to perceive more complexity in your solution than may actually be required, and as a result, may see your solution differently than an option where the path is clearly laid out.

There are three strategies the brain executes to avoid influence and resist change.[3] The first way the brain works to avoid influence is through *physical avoidance*. For example, imagine the last time a salesperson approached you at a department store like a Nordstrom or a Macy's.

"Can I help you find something?" the salesperson asks.

In a flash, in cases where you were not seeking help, you likely respond, "No thanks, I'm just looking."

While you were outside of the store, about to walk in, did you prepare for that interaction? Were you walking up and down the sidewalk thinking to yourself,

---

1   Langley, Sue. "The Neuroscience of Change: Why It's Difficult and What Makes It Easier." Langley Group Blog, 2012, blog.langleygroup.com.au/neuroscience-of-change-what-makes-change-easier/

2   "Humans Are Hard Wired to Follow the Path of Least Resistance." Neuroscience News, 21 Feb. 2017, neurosciencenews.com/path-of-least-resistance-6139/

3   P. S. Speck and M. T. Elliott, "Predictors of Advertising Avoidance in Print and Broadcast Media," Journal of Advertising 26, no. 3 (1997): 61-76.

"If that salesperson comes up to me while I'm looking for a new pair of shoes, I need to communicate the stage that I am currently at in my purchasing journey?" Of course not! Unless you came into the store with a specific question, then that response was probably automatic.

The second core way the brain works to avoid influence is through *mechanical avoidance*, which can look like fast forwarding through commercials or filtering and deleting unwanted spam emails without reading them.

And the third way is through *cognitive avoidance*, which is the act of looking away from an influencing message, subconsciously looking away from advertisements in a magazine, newspaper, a billboard as you drive down the highway, or emails in your inbox, while rapidly honing in on the messages that feel desirable to open. Cable/satellite and paid streaming services have gained momentum not only because of their enhanced content, but also because they have less commercials, requiring less cognitive avoidance.

You can probably see where this concept is headed, from a selling perspective. While we are focused on influencing change, the approach we take must account for the buying brain's inherent wiring designed to resist.

2 - OUR BRAINS ARE WIRED TO MAKE DECISIONS WITH EMOTION AND FEELINGS, THEN JUSTIFY THOSE DECISIONS FOR THEMSELVES AND TO THE OUTSIDE WORLD USING LOGIC.

Throughout my career, the majority of sales training and enablement has been focused on teaching sellers to succeed using approaches steeped in "logic." Logic is a focus on facts, data, reasoning, proof, and evidence.

For decision making, logic is only used for the purposes of *justification* of a decision. While still important to learn and communicate, as logic plays an important role in the sales process, we are all wired to make decisions with feeling.

A feeling is a subjective point of view: an emotional state or sensation. Dr. David Rock created a model for the feelings that drive decisions that focused on humans' tendencies to move (a) towards a reward, or (b) away from risk.[4] He calls it his "SCARF" model, consisting of five domains of feelings contributing to a decision: Status, Certainty, Autonomy, Relatedness, and/or Fairness.[5]

- **Status** is about relative importance of the purchase to others. Will this purchase impact the perception others have of the buyer or their organization in a positive manner?
- **Certainty** is related to how well the buyer feels he or she can predict the experience that they will have as a result of the purchase. Transparency touches this domain more strongly than any other. How confident is the buyer in their forecast of what the pros and cons of a decision will be?
- **Autonomy** related to the perception that the buyer has a sense of control. Does the buyer feel as though they are gaining or losing control in their environment through this purchase?
- **Relatedness** is associated with cause and effect, or connectedness. Will this purchase have the intended consequences the buyer expects or desires?
- **Fairness** is a perception of the cost versus the expected value in return resulting from a purchase. Does the buyer believe that the anticipated results of a purchase equal or exceed the anticipated expense in terms of the price, time, and risk associated with making such a purchase?

In my research, I was stunned by the discoveries of individuals who, due to brain damage to specific regions in the brain, lost their ability to generate feelings like those outlined above. And, as a result, these individuals actually lost the ability to make decisions!

---

4   Rock, David. Understanding David Rock's SCARF Model. 2014, conference.iste.org/uploads/ISTE2016/HANDOUTS/KEY_100525149/understandingtheSCARFmodel.pdf

5   SCARF: A brain-based model for collaborating with and influencing others. First published in the *NeuroLeadership Journal*, Issue one, 2008.

In the book, *Descartes' Error*, author and neuroscientist Antonio Damasio takes readers on his journey of coming to this discovery, that without feelings, decisions could no longer be made.[6]

One such subject was an individual he refers to as "Eliot." Eliot was by all indications a good father and husband, enjoyed the respect and admiration of his peers, and had a great job. Then, Eliot began to have headaches, followed by blurred vision, and a visit to the doctor that ended with a diagnosis of a benign brain tumor.

During the successful surgery to remove this tumor, portions of brain tissue damaged by this tumor had to be removed as well.

Following the surgery, while Eliot appeared on the outside to be normal, something else happened. This "something" caused his wife and children to leave him, and led to the end of his career as well as the eventual squandering of every last dollar he had.

Damasio reached Eliot, living on a friend's couch, penniless. As Damasio worked with him, Eliot described his situation, the loss of family, friends, homes, and money without emotion. Eliot seemed to show no disdain or concern for his situation.

He could no longer decide to get out of bed in the morning. He could no longer prioritize tasks. Eliot was still great with numbers, and did well at using logic to solve problems and tackle tasks with specific instructions. However, making decisions on anything from what clothes to wear to what to have for lunch to prioritizing was now impossible. Why did all of this happen to Eliot? As it turns out, due to the damage done to the limbic system, Eliot lost the ability to make decisions.

---

6   Antonio Damasio, Descartes' Error (New York: Penguin Books, Reprint edition 2005).

From Damasio's research, a connection was made between an individual's inability to experience feelings with their loss of decision-making capacity. Damasio proclaimed, "We are not thinking machines that feel. We are feeling machines that think." Before these breakthrough studies, as he writes in his book, we were all taught that "emotions and reason did not mix any more than oil and water."

If we as sales professionals don't paint a picture to inspire differentiated feelings for the buyer, the buyers will paint their own picture. And, when they do, if that picture is not the correct one, you lose. Are you helping to paint the specific picture of how a buyer will experience status, certainty, autonomy, relatedness, or fairness?

3 - HUMAN BEINGS MAKE OVER 90% OF OUR DECISIONS SUBCONSCIOUSLY.

In typical sales processes, the focus is on getting the buyer through their decision-making process in an attempt to maximize the odds that the buyer makes a purchase from you. While that's a fantastic goal, we often forget that the sales process isn't about one decision, but hundreds (or maybe even thousands) of subconscious micro-decisions.

Branding expert Martin Lindstrom concluded that we make as many as 10,000 decisions per day, and the majority (>90%) are made subconsciously.[7]

In one of Lindstrom's studies, which reveals our subconscious decision making, he studied 2,080 smokers on their perceptions of the warning labels that appear on the side of packs of cigarettes. The Cigarette Labeling and Advertising Act of 1965 obliged cigarette companies to include warning labels on all cigarette packages.[8] While the requirements for cigarette manufacturers changed over time, the

---

7   "90 Percent Of All Purchasing Decisions Are Made Subconsciously." ISPO News Magazine, Jan. 2015, mag.ispo.com/2015/01/90-percent-of-all-purchasing-decisions-are-made-subconsciously/?lang=en

8   "Public Health Information." R.J. Reynolds Tobacco Company, www.rjrt.com/tobacco-use-health/public-health-information/

purpose of these warning labels was designed to expose consumers to the dangers of cigarette smoking and extended tobacco use. In some countries, the labels feature grotesque pictures of individuals suffering from the negative effects of tobacco.

During pre-interviews with the participants of his study, smokers were asked about their perceptions of the warning labels, the label's impact on their desire to have a cigarette, and their desire to quit smoking. In almost every interview, participants communicated the negative feelings those labels generated associated with cigarette smoking, with those participants consistently communicating verbally a desire to stop smoking.

Following the pre-interview, participants were then connected to their brain through a functional magnetic resonance imaging (fMRI) machine. The fMRI is a technique for measuring and mapping brain activity that is noninvasive and safe.[9] Participants, once connected, were shown cigarette warning labels, while this fMRI device allowed Lindstrom and his team to measure the brain activity associated with decision making. The results were staggering.

Cigarette warning labels caused smokers to subconsciously desire a cigarette. The warning labels had the opposite effect on smokers than was intended. The warning labels activated "craving spots" in the brain, resulting in smokers wanting to smoke more, not less. Lindstrom's findings resulted in his conclusion that, "You really can't ask that question to the conscious mind and depend on a verbal answer."[10]

As sales professionals configuring our message, we so often believe that our prospecting messages of massive returns, incredible growth, and huge profit margins will compel your audience to action. The human brain does not always equate what's best for it with the actions and decisions it makes.

---

9   http://fmri.ucsd.edu/Research/whatisfmri.html

10   Martin Lindstrom, *Buy-ology* (New York: Doubleday, 2008), 7-16.

KEEPERS

World-class sales professionals must be skilled in a host of specialties including researching, prospecting, positioning, quarterbacking, presenting, and negotiating. In each specialty, the goal is to drive buyer decisions. In this first foundational chapter, you gained a core understanding of how the brain's decision-making engine functions. Again, the three core truths of decision making which will be referred to throughout the rest of the book are:

- **Our brains are designed to resist "influence:"** Our brains put up barriers to block themselves from being unduly driven to make decisions and change.
- **Our brains are wired to make decisions with emotion and feelings, then justify those decisions for themselves and to the outside world using logic:** Logic is the backup for a decision, not the driver of the decision.
- **Human beings make over 90% of decisions subconsciously:** As individuals, we are in a constant state of decision making. You're not just building towards one purchase decision, you're influencing countless decisions with every buyer interaction.

CHAPTER TWO

BUYER EMPATHY

"Transparency is the risk, authenticity the currency, and trust is the reward."
—Dr. Mani

CLOSE YOUR EYES. JUST KIDDING...THIS IS A BOOK, SO YOU'D better keep them open. But let's start over for a moment, and with your eyes open, imagine you've just traveled back to the year 1910.

You hold a commission-only sales job, which was very common at the time. Actually, you are more like an agent for the company whose products you sell. In other words, if you don't sell anything this week, you go home with nothing. Sink or swim.

You are your buyers' only source of information on the products and services that you sell. There is no internet. There are no computers. There are no smart phones. Even wired telephones aren't pervasive yet.

There are competitors, but none of them are in your same location. Mass airplane travel won't begin for almost forty years. UPS is just getting started out on the West Coast, acting as a messenger service (often for the US Postal Service, ironically enough). In other words, there is practically no competition.

As the seller, you have all of the control.

As the only source of information on your product, you can afford to be aggressive. After all, revealing a product's flaws may mean you'd have to skip a meal next week. Better to ask for forgiveness later. How "transparent" would you be?

In this case, your inherent survival mechanism in taking caring of yourself and your family is likely to trump your morals and values, right?

In this environment, buyers learn the hard way how much they can truly trust the sellers. Mistrust of the sales profession was enforced, re-enforced, then stigmatized.

If you had your eyes closed, you can go ahead and open them now.

Depending on the study you read, in most industries, approximately 25% of all deals that are truly "qualified" actually close, where a "qualified" opportunity is one which meets the criteria you and your company have defined, indicating that the potential customer is worth pursuing.

I wasn't a math major in college, but that means 75% of your qualified leads do not result in a sale. And, according to a research study by "The Sales Benchmark Index," a whopping 58% of qualified opportunities end with the buyer opting to do nothing. Time has been wasted by both the buyer and you, the seller. The opportunity cost of working an opportunity that doesn't pan out versus you spending time looking for, cultivating and winning with a buyer who will change with you can be substantial. Why does this happen? So often, it's due to the homework the buyer has done beyond you and beyond the claims of your direct interactions.

THE HIGHER THE TRUST, THE LESS HOMEWORK FOR THE BUYER

Do you build bulletproof trust during your interactions with the prospective buyers you work with? During every interaction with a potential buyer, your buyer is subconsciously assessing whether you are communicating with sincerity, competence, and consistency. If the second the buyer's brain senses insincerity, ineptitude, or inconsistency, their brain's "uh oh" alarm will sound off subconsciously.

Uncertainty leads to "homework" for the buyer. When the buyer loses even minute amounts of confidence in the feeling they have regarding the decision they are making or the justification they'll need to execute on a decision, they are driven to do research beyond the information and feeling you, the seller, have provided. Every interaction you have with the buyer is either building trust and confidence, or eroding it, without you even realizing you're doing it. And, the more homework you require your potential buyer to do, (a) the less control you have over your opportunity, (b) the longer the sales cycle will take for the buyer to reach a buying decision, and (c) the more likely your qualified opportunity will result in the dreaded "no decision."

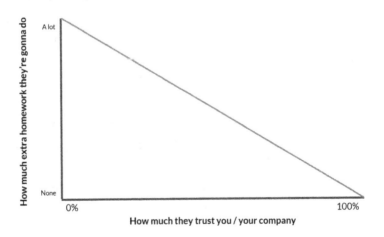

Think about it. When you have full, 100% trust in the person guiding you through your decision, whatever it may be, you are less inclined to look elsewhere to fill in the gaps. And, in the situations where you have less than 100% trust and look elsewhere to get to your required level of comfort, you often don't come back to the seller. In a sales cycle, how many times have you lost a deal where your client presents you with information you wish they hadn't found?

Often times, as sellers, we'll hear feedback from a buyer like:

"Because you don't have the feature we need, we're going to go with one of your competitors."

"I spoke to a couple of peers about your solution, and their experience tells me we're better off re-prioritizing/going in a different direction."

"I found some information on your solution that makes us uncomfortable with a purchase right now."

In many cases, we won't get *any* feedback on why we lost. The client will have just gone silent. Or, we'll receive an email saying something like, "We're going down a different path," or "We don't have the budget," or "We're putting off the purchase until later in the year." Sometimes, they are telling the truth. More often than not, the true reason is never shared.

For example, think of a time when you are making a purchase online, and the retailer you're visiting doesn't display both positive and negative reviews on their own website. In those instances, a high percentage of consumers looking to make a high consideration purchase did further research outside of that specific retailer's site. It's likely you would, too. In a PowerReviews study, here's where they went:[1]

---

1   PowerReviews 2016 Path to Purchase Study. https://www.powerreviews.com/wp-content/uploads/2016/06/Path-to-Purchase-Whitepaper061716.pdf

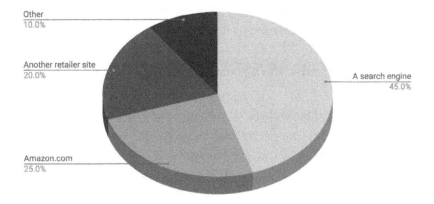

Other
10.0%

Another retailer site
20.0%

A search engine
45.0%

Amazon.com
25.0%

In many cases, the consumer would leave the website they were browsing to do this additional research and never come back. Just having one review on a product page increased the odds of conversion (a sale) by 65%.[2] Why? Because transparency wins. Because the retailer is displaying transparency through the mere act of allowing consumers to share their experiences on their own site, the buyers feel confident that they have the information they need to make a decision.

And, that same study shows that among shoppers under the age of forty-five, 86% purposely seek out negative reviews before making a purchase.

Bringing this concept back to our world of "business-to-business" sales, in order for buyers to create the necessary feeling to make a highly confident decision, maintaining control through the decision process is key. Your buyer is interacting with you, not a website. In e-commerce, it's called "maximizing conversions;" every website visitor is a qualified prospect, and the goal is keep those visitors on their site until a purchase is made. Your goal through building

---

2   PowerReviews study - Based on a representative sample of 14,000+ products across 100+ retailers in the PowerReviews Network that went from 0 reviews (for a minimum of 30 days) to >0 reviews (for a minimum of 30 days) over a six-month period. Traffic (impressions), sales (dollar value of orders), and conversion were measured and averaged daily for each product, then averaged by merchant and across the network.

trust should be the same, where the buyer sees you as the source of everything their brain needs to feel confident in a purchase. They don't look elsewhere. And, they don't leave you without a commitment.

WHERE TO START: INVESTIGATE WHERE THE BUYER WILL RESEARCH

So, where will your buyers look for the information they need to establish a decision when they're not getting it from you? This is a vitally important question. Achieving and maintaining 100% trust between you and your potential buyer is an impossible bar to meet all of the time, so your buyers will do some level of homework.

The higher the amount of "consideration" a buyer needs to complete a purchase, the more their brain requires transparency.[3] If you're buying generic office supplies like paper or staplers, you are more likely to decide on a brand based on the certainty associated with your familiarity with the options, your confidence in the brand, the fairness associated with the price, an advertisement you were exposed to, or some other emotion balanced against the low risk associated with a potential bad purchase. However, in a high consideration purchase like a piece of technology or equipment fundamental to your business, decisions will still be based on feeling, but the bar is higher for what the brain will require to feel confident enough to make a purchase. That confidence bar will also require more logic for the justification of the feeling.

And, with high consideration purchases, you are no longer selling to just one individual: Those organizations have buying teams, processes requiring multiple approvals, and multiple "buyers" who will need to have their brains feeling confident in finalizing a purchase with you.

For example, if you're selling a piece of equipment to a manufacturer, you can

---

3   From Reviews to Revenue, PowerReviews, 2015, spiegel.medill.northwestern.edu/_pdf/ Online%20Reviews%20Whitepaper.pdf

predict that the buying team will likely look up independent reports reviewing the pros and cons of every available alternative.

In the technology space, it could be analysts like Gartner or Forrester, or it could be online B2B feedback sites like G2Crowd or TrustRadius. If you're a corporate recruiter, it could be the reviews and ratings on a site like Glassdoor. It could be Google. It could be sites online you have never even heard of. The goal is to find out what is being said about your products, solutions, or company.

Another source of feedback your buyers will research is in talking to your current customers. Do you regularly survey your current customers? Have you done an NPS (Net Promoter Score) type survey? That data will be important, too, as your prospects reaching out behind-the-scenes to your customers could be an important channel your buyers will use.

What can you find? What would influence you if you were buying from you? Search like a buyer. This will be important information for the rest of your efforts.

KEEPERS

In this, the second foundational chapter, there are three primary takeaways you'll want to understand:

- **Every single interaction is a decision point for the buyer:** When trust is eroded, the buyer's brain will seek to either (a) figure you out, or (b) disappear into a "no-decision," a win for the competitor, or silence.
- **The less trust the buyer has in you, the more homework they will do:** When a buyer feels as though they're not getting the entire picture from you and your organization, they won't be able to make a decision without doing homework. Homework, in the form of reference checks, research through independent analysts, their own network of peers and partners, and internet searches.

- **Know where buyers will go to do their homework, and know what they will find:** Maintaining a 100% level of trust with a client is unlikely, so knowing where your buyers will look in their research is vital. Understanding what they will find will be used in your positioning and presenting.

CHAPTER THREE

WHY DOING IT RIGHT MATTERS – THE RESULTS FORMULA

"It was my understanding there would be no math."
—Chevy Chase playing Gerald Ford on
"Saturday Night Live," October 16th, 1976

T HE ACCOMPLISHED WRITER AND SPEAKER SETH GODIN ONCE painted a perfect analogy for accomplishing more each year in a talk he gave. He asked the audience to raise their right hand as high as they could, and the audience obliged. Every hand in the audience was up high. Then, he asked everyone to raise their hands a little higher. As you might imagine, everyone was able to do so.

In sales, we're asked to do everything we can to achieve maximum performance each year, similar to Seth asking the audience to raise their hand as high as they could. Then, at the beginning of the following year, we're asked to do even more. Quotas are higher. It's not as easy as simply raising your hand a little higher. However, 20%+ growth is possible with small, incremental improvements to your approach and mindset. Transparency and brain science can get you there.

I was taught very early in my career that "what gets measured gets done." As a sales leader, I always believed that the answer to, "Should we try this?" laid in the ability to measure the impact of trying it through quantified metrics. While in my last role, I wanted to measure everything to the point where my sales operations leader likely wanted to go into hiding following each quarter.

What do you measure when it comes to your sales performance? In sales, much of our focus has to do with the achievement of goals, both short-term and long-term. Our goal attainment impacts our job security, our paycheck, our opportunities for advancement, and potentially our quality of life. We all have goals, typically in the form of a quota. For example, you might say to yourself, "I want to attain or exceed my quota of $300,000 in closed-won new business this quarter." You don't simply receive a quota, then do what you've always done: periodically check your progress, get to the milestone date, check your results in your CRM system (customer relationship management), and say to yourself, "Oh, crap! I didn't make it!" You measure your activities. You understand the key metrics that will contribute to your achievement. You control your destiny.

Have you ever been on a diet? Have you ever known anyone to have gone on one? (It would be really odd if you said "no" to both...but if you did, trust me on this next analogy!) Think about the last time you did. You probably set a weight loss goal for yourself. Say, "I want to lose ten pounds in the next three months."

Now, did you just do what you've always done, but this time, you simply checked the scale a little more often? Then, at the milestone date, did you then look down at the scale and say to yourself, "Oh, crap! I didn't achieve my goal"?

Or, did you actually pay attention to your activities, your inputs and activity output, and calculate a path to reach your goal? Did you count calories, carb intake, fat and protein levels, and measure your exercise activity? If you did, would you agree that you are MUCH more likely to have achieved your goal weight?

To reach our goals, we must know what the key inputs are to our success, then measure those inputs. Understanding and measuring those components must be a core function of our lives as professional sellers.

As it turns out, there are four fundamental components that are the contributors to your actual results, and they all happen to be directly impacted by your approach through transparency:

1.   Number of Qualified Opportunities – the number of opportunities that meet your organization's criteria of a worthy opportunity to pursue.

2.   Average Deal Size – the average dollar value of each opportunity that ended in a sale.

3.   Win Rate – the percentage of qualified opportunities won versus those lost.

4.   Cycle Length – the number of days from the first meaningful interaction to the date the opportunity closed in your favor.

Under each, there are more things you can measure and calculate. However, those components are the four that contribute to your results. Simply put, if you multiply the number of qualified opportunities times your average deal size, times your win rate, and then divide it by the cycle length, you have your results.

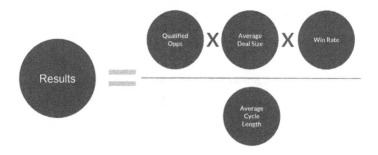

Fig. 3.1. The Results Formula

Here comes the math. Regardless what your numbers are, getting 20%+ growth seems relatively easy when you see it as just these components. **If you increase your number of qualified opportunities by 5%, your average deal size by 5%, your win rate by 5%, and you shrink your cycle length by 5%, you will grow your results by 22%.**

1. If you have twenty qualified opportunities over the period being measured, growing that by 5% is simply adding one more qualified opportunity.

2. If you have an average deal size of $20,000, growing that by 5% is simply raising your average deal size to $21,000.

3. If your win rate is currently 25%, growing that by 5% is simply raising your win rate to 26.25%.

4. If your cycle length is typically sixty days, shrinking that by three days to an average of fifty-seven days is a 5% improvement.

Do all four together, and you'll raise your results by 22%. The math works with any combination of numbers. Trust me, I've done them. I've unsuccessfully tried to break this formula.

Transparency has a way of influencing each of the metrics that contribute most directly to these results. If done right, during every interaction—from your prospecting outreach to the way you negotiate—you will find that:

- Your **number of qualified opportunities will go up**, as you are more likely to meet and exceed client expectations, increasing your client satisfaction metrics, and thus your referrals will go up;
- Through transparent negotiations, your customers will share in configuring the deal, which will result in **larger deal sizes**;
- Your **win rates will go up** dramatically because you'll be making it very hard for your competitors to position against you, and you will work better opportunities by more effectively leaving the loser deals at the starting line; and
- Your **cycle lengths will decline** due to your prospects' reduction in need to do their own homework.

WHAT TO DO WITH THE RESULTS FORMULA?

Ensure you have a tight, consistent definition of a "qualified" opportunity. For each opportunity, I tend to like to "take the prospect's TEMP," focusing on the following factors:

T – **Trigger**

E – **Engagement**

M – **Mobilizer**

P – **Plan**

Trigger: When I refer to the trigger, I refer to the point where the buyer has recognized that their status quo is no longer sustainable. Is something occurring in the buyer's world that has them committed to making a change? Whether we've created that trigger or not, this is also known as the "compelling event" or the understanding of what happens if a change does not occur.

Engagement: When looking at engagement, I am asking myself: Is the customer/prospect engaged? Have we scheduled a next step or follow up? Evidence of a qualified opportunity is shown in the customer's willingness to set aside time in their calendar and start the buying journey with you. If they say they'll "call you next week" or you have to chase them down, you don't have the customer's engagement.

Mobilizer: Have we connected with the individual or individuals capable of 'mobilizing' an organization to make a change? A term coined by the team at CEB, mobilizers are individuals who have the trust and confidence of executives in their organization, and are capable of actually making change happen within an organization.[1]

Plan: The plan refers to how far you are in drafting a mutual decision plan (MDP) with your prospect. Have we had the discussion with the buyer around what steps will be required to fix the problem with their status quo? Have they contributed to outlining the plan? Qualification is strong when your buyer will collaborate with you on the formation of a mutual decision plan.

Together, TEMP serves as a constant beacon for a qualified opportunity. All of the elements of TEMP are subject to change during the buying journey, however, Engagement has always served as a key indicator of progress. A client may have a Trigger driving them to change, you may have a clearly identified Mobilizer you are working with, and have a mutual Plan in place, however, Engagement is a constant. Are you on their calendar?

Establish a baseline:

Qualified Opportunities: Using your definition of a qualified opportunity, review the number of qualified opportunities you've had month-to-month or quarter-to-quarter over the past 12-24 months. Determine the volume of

---

1   Brent Adamson et al., *The Challenger Customer* (New York: Penguin, 2015), 35-56.

opportunities you can conceivably manage at any one time. (i.e., If you have a large number of high velocity, lower dollar value opportunities, then a month-to-month view would be ideal. If you have a small number of longer cycle, high dollar value opportunities, measuring the baseline over a longer period of time would be ideal.)

Average Deal Sizes: What is the dollar value average for the opportunities you have won? These are a better representative of your typical clients than those that were qualified but ultimately did not purchase anything.

Win Rate: What is the percentage of qualified opportunities which resulted in a win? Be realistic. Are there opportunities where the client is no longer engaged, has pushed off a decision, or others which no longer fit your criteria for a qualified opportunity? Mark those as lost for your calculations.

Cycle Lengths: What is the average cycle length for the opportunities you have won? The start date for your cycle length measure should align with the date when the opportunity became *mutually* active. For example, an opportunity where the buyer requested you follow up in six months should not be considered active during that period of time.

Measure your progress: Every month, put a reminder in your calendar to measure your progress. What are the percentage lifts or reductions in each category? If your goals require a lift in performance by say, 20%, are your results in the four categories giving you the required lift to get there?

Peter Drucker, widely known as the person who invented modern management, often was heard saying, "If you can't measure it, you can't improve it." Feeling as though a change you are making is having a positive impact is nice, but the data will provide you with the logic to justify those assumptions.

KEEPERS

In the third foundational chapter, the three primary takeaways are:

- **The Results Formula:** Your results are made up of four KPIs, (1) your number of qualified opportunities, (2) your average deal sizes, (3) your win rates, and (4) your sales cycle lengths. Incremental improvements in all four categories add up to sharp improvements in your overall results.
- **Taking the buyer's TEMP:** Clearly defining your organization's criteria for what constitutes a qualified opportunity is important for your calculations to work. TEMP is the criteria I use, made up of a Trigger event, Engagement proven by a buyer's willingness to put you on their calendar, a Mobilizer who is able to make change within an organization, and a Plan mutually discussed outlining the decision-making journey.
- **Know your numbers, know what works:** If you know your numbers, you can quickly access the impact of changes.

CHAPTER FOUR

WHY CHANGE, WHY YOU, WHY NOW?

"If you always do what you've always done,
you'll always get what you've always got."
– Anonymous

N ORDER TO APPLY TRANSPARENCY TO SELLING EFFECTIVELY, WE must answer the following questions: What does a salesperson really do? What are they actually responsible for?

Ultimately, the success or failure of a company is in its ability to effectively sell its products and services. A sale is an outcome. If your product is weak, but salespeople are still able to sell those products, your company will stay in business, at least in the short term. If the economy is struggling and customer budgets are tight, but salespeople are able to find ways to motivate customers to spend on your products, your company will stay in business. If your management team is weak, but your sales team is strong and able to sell your products and services into the market despite the company's poor leadership, your company will stay in business. For better or worse, a company's success is determined greatly by how it sells.

To start, most organizations outline what they call their "sales process." The goal of a documented sales process was originally proposed as a proven step-by-step approach, with standardized scripts at each stage, ensuring everyone on the sales team was saying the same thing, conveying the same messages, and using consistent tools aligned to the steps. The theory before the advent of the internet was that by modeling a successful sales process, the documented sales process would allow the company to plug in practically any salesperson, train them to follow the steps, and achieve optimal consistent results in a predictable fashion.

However, the digital age has made selling a "buyer's market," where a buyer has the upper hand in establishing their feelings around a potential purchase before they ever talk to you. A sales-activity-focused checklist must now be grounded in the fact that our potential buyers are at different stages in determining how your product or service could fit into their lives. We must rethink the traditional sales process, and consider each activity with the buyer in mind.

THE CONCEPT OF PRIORITY

As much as you may try, you can't control people's priorities, but you *can* use brain science to understand how they form those priorities.

A buyer's reptilian brain is thinking about self-preservation. This desire for self-preservation is shaped by the challenges and tasks they face at home and at work. They have objectives they have to meet at work, which ensure they keep their job, get paid, achieve bonuses, and help them progress towards whatever their career objectives happen to be. Many are short-term thinkers who would struggle to tell you what their career desires are, even two years out. They want to get through the day, through the week, and to the weekend to spend time decompressing, hanging with family, friends, or alone on a boat with a fishing pole in hand.

Their priorities are not your priorities, and never will be. Where you see a return on investment, a big step for their business, and a lift in perception, they see a project, a risk, and uncertainty. But without trust, the rock being pushed up the hill becomes an asteroid.

Every single buyer you talk to has piles of problems, both small and large. I have worked for or consulted with many companies, and have held senior roles at a few. At any given moment, I was faced with more problems than I could solve. Like all executives, I had a finite amount of time, a finite budget, and a finite set of resources who could be deployed to address those problems. Almost every salesperson who reached out to me and our company was offering a solution that could probably address one of them and generate a ROI.

The key isn't convincing a potential buyer that your solution has significant ROI. That's logical, but not emotional. And, given that every problem an executive faces can't all be solved at once, these problems need to be prioritized before decisions are made. Typically, a buyer can only concentrate on fixing three to five problems at a time.

Which ones are they? That depends on the feeling your buyer has about the problem they are addressing, and the perceived effort to address those problems. The types of questions that buyers often ask themselves are regarding which problems to address are:

- Which are going to make the biggest impact, whose effort won't require a nightmarish effort?
- Which problems will help my internal reputation (my boss, my peers, my team)?
- Which do I feel would give me the best shot of attaining my bonus?
- Which are least likely to require that I work over the weekend, as my spouse hates unexpected plan changes?

In other words, which projects do I really believe will increase revenue, reduce cost, or help me avoid a direct hit from a freight train, with the highest return on perceived effort? Which can I do while assuming the lowest amount of perceived risk? Risk, in terms of investment, level of effort for the business, and what happens if the project fails.

Buyers can find themselves in one of three stages:

1. **Actively Buying (AB)** = In this stage, the buyer already understands the cost of *not* making a change to their current environment, has identified and prioritized a problem, and is actively seeking a solution. ABs will often "commoditize" your products and services against the alternatives they're looking at by lumping solutions together that, from their outside perspective, look similar. Often, they'll look at a website or two to determine what their requirements "should" be, then select the vendor who meets the minimum acceptable criteria, at the lowest cost. As you'll see in the chart below, the number of ABs is small relative to the entire base of prospects you could pursue.

2. **Passively Buying (PB)** = A potential buyer recognizes that a problem exists but has yet to prioritize resolving it. At home, I look around and see all sorts of things I could fix. The fence in the backyard needs paint. The handle on our dishwasher is broken. I'm aware of these problems, but they aren't on the top of the list of priorities for me to fix right now. In these circumstances, a buyer may be willing to listen to you, willing to engage, however it hasn't made it up to the top of their prioritization list. The book *Absolute Value* refers to these individuals and companies as "Couch Tracking," meaning that they are passively looking for better ways to solve a problem, which means paying attention to you and the market without actually doing much.[1]

3. **Status Quo (SQ)** = This kind of buyer is fully content with their current situation, regardless of how much better their situation may become if they

---

1   Itamar Simonson and Emanuel Rosen, *Absolute Value* (New York: HarperCollins, 2014), 35.

pursue an alternative. They are often unaware of a better way, or perfectly satisfied with their approach. It's like an accounting department using graph paper and long math to manage their organization's books, or like a buddy of mine who is still using a flip phone instead of a smartphone, still printing out maps online versus investing in a smartphone with GPS. In many cases, these individuals are in denial, and are not considering alternative approaches.

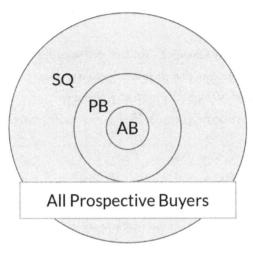

Fig. 4.1. The three buying stages.

Which one would you rather be dealing with? The ABs, who think they've figured you out, understand what they need, and are ready to compare alternatives? The PBs, who understand that they have a problem to solve, but are too busy putting out other fires to focus on it? Or, would you prefer the SQs, who believe they are satisfied with the status quo?

You'll need to deal with all three buying states, and you will need to adjust your approach for each of their feelings and emotions. I would argue that your ideal opportunity is with the SQs. Although it's up for debate, I have found that when you become the guide, educating the client on a problem or risk they didn't know they had, more often that buyer will see you as the Sherpa guiding them up the mountain from SQ to PB to AB. While your number of qualified opportunities may go down with a focus on those SQ prospects, your win rates and deal sizes will often go up.

THE CONCEPT OF WHY

The simplest way to observe the behaviors of the buyer along their journey is to think about driving clear answers to the following three questions:

Section 1: "Why Change?" To start, you want the buyer to decide through feelings and emotion that their status quo is no longer sustainable. At the end of this section of your sales process, you and your prospect should be able to mutually answer the question, "Why is a change from the current approach required?"

Section 2: "Why You?" Once the buyer has been triggered for change, the focus now is around why, if change is necessary, your company is the best path. Mutual discovery intensifies, where you are learning more about the prospect, and the prospect is actively engaged in learning about you. At the end of this section of your sales process, you and your prospect should be able to mutually answer the question, "Why (insert your company name here)?"

Section 3: "Why Now?" As the buyer has opted to go with your company's solution, you will want to drive the prospect to act now versus later. Attention turns to reviewing contracts, aligning resources, and the buying organization often pursuing final approvals.

When configuring your sales process, acquire the mindset of recognizing the state of the buyer in their purchase journey. Your efforts will still include prospecting, positioning, presenting and negotiating, but in the context of your buyer's answers to these questions: Why change, why you, and why now?

VISUALIZING THE BUYER JOURNEY / SALES PROCESS

The following graphic illustrates a selling process that is aligned with the buyer's journey and provides examples of how you can help the buyer answer the three questions:

WHY CHANGE?		WHY YOU?		WHY NOW?		
Suspect (0%)	Discover (10%)	Confirm (25%)	Decision (50%)	Selected (75%)	Negotiation (90%)	Closed Won (100%)
"Teach" Be succinctly valuable Customer is reciprocating	Trigger conceptually understood Problems / consequences of inaction conceptually understood Prioritization understood Plan configuration in process Mobilizer identified & fund path ID'd Customer is "engaged"	Document & articulate differentiators Why are we the best partner for the prospect? Agreement from customer on differentiators Customer is "engaged"	We're a finalist (1 of 2 or 3) Real time-table (trigger re-confirmed) All decision makers ID'd and engaged Real $ - no surprises Yes or No pending Customer is "engaged"	Verbally selected Only thing remaining is the paperwork Contract ready - sent to client Mutually agreed upon close plan Customer is "engaged"	Verbal agreement Round of legal completed - no deal breakers Customer is "engaged"	Received signed contracts
	4-6 weeks?	1-2 weeks?	2-4 weeks?	2-4 weeks?	2-4 weeks?	

ACTIVE PIPELINE

Fig. 4.2. An example of a sales process aligned with a buying process.

As you're attempting to penetrate the client's defense mechanism and understand whether this client is worth pursuing (versus spending your time on other client pursuits), the client is thinking, **"Why change?"** Your activities as a seller should be aligned with the focus of working the buyer through key decision #1, which is to decide that their status quo is no longer sustainable. The typical activities that are taking place in the "Why Change?" category include "Prospecting," where you are generating new opportunities, "Positioning," where you are engaging in the initial dialogue with a prospective buyer, and "Mutual Decision Plans."

As you are working through configuring a recommendation for the client, and clearly building the business case, the client is thinking, "Why you?" Your activities as a seller should now focused on making the case for you and your organization as the choice for addressing their decision in the earlier stages of the process by which they've decided to make a change to their status quo. The activities that are taking place in the "Why You?" category include "Presenting," where you are making a formal presentation and recommendation for the buyer's business, as well as assisting them in the "logic" to support their decision through the details, often including checking with "References."

And, once the buyer selects your service, he or she is constantly battling with the final checkbox of confidence in their brain. The buyer is working through the final approvals, asking themselves whether everything feels right with their choice, and whether they should really do this. Am I sure this is the best use of our funds? Am I ready to take this project on right now? What risks am I not considering? In this stage, the focus is on formalizing the relationship, working through the details of the investment, the contracts, and the terms and conditions of the agreement. It's all about "Why now?" for the buyer. In this category of the buying process, following the selection of you and your company, your focus shifts to the final "Negotiation," where the agreement on the quantity/volume of product they are purchasing from you, the price they are agreeing to pay for those products, the pricing terms, the length of commitment they will make to you and your company, along with the specific "Terms & Conditions" which will guide your partnership.

Using this approach, where you are aligning the stage of the opportunity with the specific criteria of where *they* are in their buying process, the percentages shown in Figure 4.2 above each stage align with the creation of a realistic forecast. For example, if the client is in the "Decision" stage, you will find that approximately 50% of those deals ultimately result in a win. If you're in the beginning stages of "Qualification," your odds of winning are likely around one in ten (10%). For a truly qualified deal where you're working with the buyer to answer questions and ensure full alignment in the "Confirm" stage, your odds of winning are likely around one in four (25%). And, once you've gotten into contracts and gone through a round of redlines without any deal breakers, entering the "Negotiation" stage, guess what? There's about a one in ten chance that the deal still *won't* happen.

When you multiply your deal values (how much revenue you will receive from the buyer's purchase) by those percentages, you can start to hone in on a realistic forecast without resorting to gut instinct.

The diagonal line going through the middle of Figure 4.2 is meant to represent how, in order to maintain consistent performance, you must have more opportunities at 10% than at 25%, more at 25% than at 50%, and so on. This visualization of your current pipeline will drive more accurate forecasts, more consistency in your results, and be an effective guide to the activities that drive the decisions the buyer is making at each stage in the cycle.

KEEPERS

In this final foundational chapter, the two primary takeaways are:

- **Priorities**: Recognizing that your best opportunities may begin where a client is perfectly happy with their SQ (Status Quo), and your worst opportunities may begin where your client is in an AB (Active Buying) status is important. Understanding these different states, and learning to recognize where your potential buyer is will impact your approach to prospecting, positioning, and presenting.
- **Why Change? Why You? Why Now?**: At any point in your sales process, the buyer is likely either deciding why they should change from their current solution, why they should change with you, and why they should change with you right now. Your selling activities must reflect this understanding. As we move to Section 2, we'll use these three questions as our guide.

SECTION 2:

WHY CHANGE?

CHAPTER FIVE

EMAIL PROSPECTING

D RIVING DOWN MY STREET APPROACHING MY HOUSE, I SAW TWO individuals walking up to a neighbor's door. These two individuals were well dressed, and one was holding a clipboard.

My subconscious brain was saying, "Uh, oh! Looks like these two will be making their way to our house soon to sell us something. I must warn my family!"

Without conscious processing, I felt my foot hitting the accelerator more aggressively. I quickly pulled into my garage, closing it before I even had the engine off. I ran into the house, closed the drapes, and advised my wife and kids to go upstairs, away from the front door. It was as though we were in war time, and the government was coming to take our provisions. I'm guessing I am not alone in my reaction to what many believe is the epitome of interruptive, high-pressure selling.

The popularity of another type of interruptive selling, using the telephone, began to overtake the sales world in the early 1980s. Telephone selling was seen as the new shiny way to get voice-to-voice conversations with potential buyers. Coupled with its lower cost than in-person selling and the ability to reach many more potential buyers in a shorter amount of time, the number of "telemarketing agencies" in the United States went from fifty in 1985, to over nine hundred in 1995.[1]

By 1995, telephone answering machines and voicemail expanded in use, and prospecting techniques had to change again. However, the slow deterioration of the effectiveness of outbound telephone selling started with Dr. Shirley Ann Jackson's research, which led to the creation of caller ID, among other technology. Caller ID became the equivalent of looking out your window and seeing a door-to-door salesperson coming up your driveway.[2] If you do not recognize the person, you often pretend like you're not home.

Now, email is the medium that is the most effective, efficient, and economical path to your buyers. However, advancements in email technology are beginning to have the same effect as caller ID had on the telephone call. With limited alternatives, optimizing our behavior when it comes to email outreach is the clearest area in which to focus.

EMPATHIZE WITH YOUR BUYER'S INBOX

To start, think about email as a communication medium for a moment. Why do we, as human beings, check email as often as we do?

1. **Responsiveness**: In the business world, responsiveness is an admirable trait. Think about it. It's Tuesday night, and your boss just sent you an email. You happen to see it, as the little red number pops up next to the email icon on your phone. What do you do? If you're like most people, you respond instantly. And why do you respond instantly? You may want to show your boss that you're working off hours, in hopes that she will file this experience in her brain when it comes time to tell her boss about you, put in for a promotion, or even give you a raise. At the very least, every

---

1   "Telemarketing: Overview." Ad Age, 15 Sept. 2003, adage.com/article/adage-encyclope-dia/telemarketing-overview/98900/

2   "Dr. Shirley Ann Jackson." Dr. Shirley Jackson: Telecommunications Inventions, www.black-inventor.com/Dr-Shirley-Jackson.asp

time you're responsive, you think you might be increasing your value as an employee in the eyes of your superiors.

2. **The Low Number Inbox**: How does it feel to clear out a bunch of emails from your inbox? Think about the feeling when you somehow manage to reach the height of an empty inbox, or something close to it. Your brain actually creates endorphins when you delete emails, providing a temporary high.

3. **Reward**: Checking email is like playing the instant lottery. There's a chance you're going to win. Something incredible could be sitting there, just waiting for you. All you have to do is look. But, the odds are the house is going to win...and there will be a whole lot of nothing there.

As a result, you likely check your email fairly often, with the following thoughts swirling in your subconscious mind:

1) What if there's something I need to respond to in my inbox right now?

2) What if there's big news waiting for me in my inbox right now?

3) What if there's an incredible opportunity waiting for me in my inbox right now?

Buyers' brains work just like yours. If anything above strikes a chord with you, I promise you it would strike a chord with your buyer.

BREAKING THROUGH THE INITIAL RESISTANCE

If trust is either strengthened or eroded with every interaction, consider my inbox as the CRO of PowerReviews, filled with cold emails. Here's a collection of some recent emails I received:

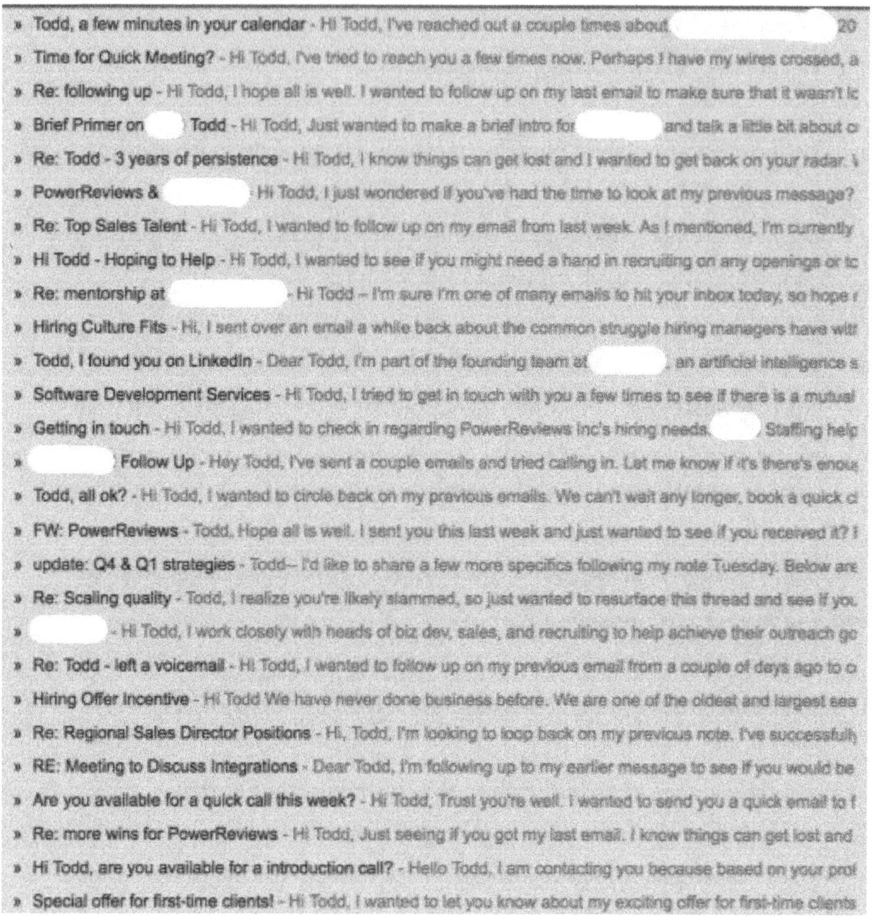

» Todd, a few minutes in your calendar - Hi Todd, I've reached out a couple times about   20
» Time for Quick Meeting? - Hi Todd, I've tried to reach you a few times now. Perhaps I have my wires crossed, a
» Re: following up - Hi Todd, I hope all is well. I wanted to follow up on my last email to make sure that it wasn't lo
» Brief Primer on   Todd - Hi Todd, Just wanted to make a brief intro for   and talk a little bit about o
» Re: Todd - 3 years of persistence - Hi Todd, I know things can get lost and I wanted to get back on your radar. I
» PowerReviews &   Hi Todd, I just wondered if you've had the time to look at my previous message?
» Re: Top Sales Talent - Hi Todd, I wanted to follow up on my email from last week. As I mentioned, I'm currently
» Hi Todd - Hoping to Help - Hi Todd, I wanted to see if you might need a hand in recruiting on any openings or to
» Re: mentorship at   - Hi Todd – I'm sure I'm one of many emails to hit your inbox today, so hope t
» Hiring Culture Fits - Hi, I sent over an email a while back about the common struggle hiring managers have with
» Todd, I found you on LinkedIn - Dear Todd, I'm part of the founding team at   , an artificial intelligence s
» Software Development Services - Hi Todd, I tried to get in touch with you a few times to see if there is a mutual
» Getting in touch - Hi Todd, I wanted to check in regarding PowerReviews Inc's hiring needs.   Staffing help
»   Follow Up - Hey Todd, I've sent a couple emails and tried calling in. Let me know if it's there's enou
» Todd, all ok? - Hi Todd, I wanted to circle back on my previous emails. We can't wait any longer, book a quick c
» FW: PowerReviews - Todd, Hope all is well. I sent you this last week and just wanted to see if you received it? I
» update: Q4 & Q1 strategies - Todd– I'd like to share a few more specifics following my note Tuesday. Below are
» Re: Scaling quality - Todd, I realize you're likely slammed, so just wanted to resurface this thread and see if you
»   - Hi Todd, I work closely with heads of biz dev, sales, and recruiting to help achieve their outreach go
» Re: Todd - left a voicemail - Hi Todd, I wanted to follow up on my previous email from a couple of days ago to o
» Hiring Offer Incentive - Hi Todd We have never done business before. We are one of the oldest and largest sea
» Re: Regional Sales Director Positions - Hi, Todd, I'm looking to loop back on my previous note. I've successfully
» RE: Meeting to Discuss Integrations - Dear Todd, I'm following up to my earlier message to see if you would be
» Are you available for a quick call this week? - Hi Todd, Trust you're well. I wanted to send you a quick email to f
» Re: more wins for PowerReviews - Hi Todd, Just seeing if you got my last email. I know things can get lost and
» Hi Todd, are you available for a introduction call? - Hello Todd, I am contacting you because based on your prof
» Special offer for first-time clients! - Hi Todd, I wanted to let you know about my exciting offer for first-time clients

Fig. 5.1. An actual screenshot of my inbox as the chief revenue officer of PowerReviews.

What do you see here? A couple of things to notice:

1. **The Previews:** Almost every user interface for an email inbox has a short preview of ten to fifteen words. While a great emphasis has been made on optimizing the "subject line" of your email to intrigue the recipient to open, the *preview* is where the decision your recipient is making as to whether to open your email is made.

2. **Lots of "I" Statements**: In Figure 5.1 above, every preview (except for two) makes prominent use of the word "I"(and even one implied the word "I" in starting the sentence with the word "Just"). The problem is that when you make the email about yourself, you're signaling the brain that you are attempting to influence the recipient, versus attempting to help the recipient.

3. **White Noise**: When looking at the inbox, they all appear to blend together, where no message stands out. As an executive with limited time, which message would you open? Or, would you simply 'select all' and click delete?

Which of these preview panes would communicate trust? Which strengthen it? Which erode it? Think about the "preview" as the new "caller ID." Think about the "preview" how a homeowner may look out the window to see the old door-to-door seller coming up the driveway. It's no longer just the subject line of your emails that matter. Those first few words must tell the recipient that the message is intended to influence. Otherwise, the brain will resist, delete your message, and not give it another thought.

How do we optimize those first few words of the email? Through personalization and value creation, not through sales pitches and attempts to influence.

Here are the words and messages you should avoid in the beginning of your emails:

1. **"I" or "We:"** The first sentence of a prospecting email should not be about you. Instead it must convey something of value to the person you're targeting.

2. **Meaningless pleasantries**: "How are you?" "Hope you're having a great week!" "Hope your quarter is off to a great start!" In a cold email, these generic pleasantries signal that the person is disingenuous. And, they're

taking valuable real estate in the preview.

3. **Guilt trips:** Telling me you've already emailed multiple times just reminds me why I didn't open or respond previously. Thanks!

From 2003 to 2005, I owned and operated a sales training company, and my expertise was teaching cold calling techniques. I'd like to apologize. I was wrong. It's not about the volume of calls and the metrics. It's not about making as many calls as possible. The human brain isn't wired to engage that way. Doing one hundred calls/emails with a 5% hit rate means you've successfully connected with five people. Doing thirty calls with a 30% hit rate means you've successfully connected with nine people. And, if done correctly, those nine will have a higher conversion rate into qualified pipeline. The same mindset applies to emails.

Prospecting can be awful when it becomes solely about the metrics and ratios, and not about what it is meant to be. Prospecting is the first step in building fruitful, meaningful, mutually beneficial relationships with people. People. Human beings. Human beings who get paid to do a job and hit their personal KPIs (key performance indicators), put food on the table and enjoy life when the work day is done.

Prospecting is disruptive. When you email, your potential buyer isn't sitting at their desk, staring on their inbox, exclaiming, "Come on, email! I sure hope a salesperson sends me a note regarding why I should buy from them!"

Take this opportunity to stand out from the crowd through transparency and effective communication. Spend the time to get to know your buyer, and make sure that your research is apparent in that fifteen-word window. Those are the emails that get read. Something in the email preview pane must communicate personalization and value.

When you're about to send a prospecting email, empathize! How many words are in your subject line? Then, doing simple math, subtract that from fifteen. Once you have that answer, look at that number of words that begin your email body. Those are your money makers.

And, just as importantly, your subject line and first few words must be a reflection of the content of the email itself. Otherwise, trust is immediately eroded.

CONTENT MINDSET AND THE BUYER'S BRAIN

It is likely that your prospect's entire life is online. Look for them on LinkedIn and read whatever content they have shared about their work and interests. They probably post to personal accounts, at the very least, on social networks like Twitter. Find them and follow them. It's a Google search away. I promise you, I have not cracked the code on the perfect cold call or email approach. However, if we apply what we know about transparency and brain science, we can change the way we think about email as a communication medium, and optimize its effectiveness.

	Generic	Personalized
Pitching your Products	F	C
Providing Value / No Pitch	B	A

Fig. 5.2 - Matrix showing your email prospecting "grade" based on its content.

For each email you send, consider Figure 5.2 as a guide. Are you personalizing the content of the email to the individual, or are you sending a "batch and blast" email, where every recipient receives the exact same content. Also, try to think of your emails as informative instead of purely sales-oriented. Are you educating the reader, or are you simply trying to sell them something? The perfect email is personalized and valuable, and does not feel like a pitch. It's an "A" on the Figure 5.2 grading scale.

Remember, your prospects are likely SQs (set in their Status Quo). This means that they are happy with whatever they're doing, even if there are better ways to do it. If prospecting is just an exercise in scraping the ABs (Active Buyers), your results will be disappointing.

If you want to get someone interested in you and what you have to offer, the first step is to show them you are interested in them. To show them you are interested in them, you must *actually* be interested in them. **Consider your emails an opportunity to connect, develop rapport, and start the process of educating a prospect out of their Status Quo (SQ) and into a Passive Buying state (PB), then an Active Buying state (AB).**

Here are some ways to score an "A" from Figure 5.2, providing value in a personalized way, minus the sales pitch:

1. Share information about the recipient's competitor. "Here's a quick excerpt of an interview I found with the CEO of ABC Company talking about their product development roadmap."

2. Share information that connects with their personal values. "Found this study on how the compensation plans for SVP's of finance are changing." In this case, your recipient is the SVP of finance. Compensation studies are interesting to just about everyone who gets paid to do a job.

3. Share information about something useful for their role. For example, I was sent a prospecting email from a company I had not previously known that simply had two sentences. The first read, "Here is a link to a PowerPoint

template you can use to present your quarterly metrics during your next board meeting." The second read, "Here is a link to a Sales Handbook template you can use as a starting point to build your own, or for ideas to help enhance your current version." No information about who they are or what they do. While only personalized in that they knew I was a CRO, it was highly valuable and did not contain a pitch. I used both templates, researched their company on my own, and while our company did not require their services at the time, we would certainly call them first if the need arose.

4. Offer to make a connection. Do you know other people in similar roles, where a relationship between that individual and your prospect could be mutually valuable...for them? In what way? Many of the most successful sales professionals I've known through my career are connectors. They add value through helping individuals learn from their peers, and building their networks.

5. Congratulate them. While there's a line between being genuinely interested in the person you are targeting for your products versus being creepy, I'm an advocate for congratulating people for major accomplishments: promotions, completing an ironman triathlon, having a baby, or other major life events that matter.

Again, the relationship either builds or erodes with every interaction. Personalized and valuable wins, and proving that in the fifteen-word window is your doorway in...your caller ID.

EMAIL STRUCTURE

Have you ever opened an email, and burst into tears because of its length? Me, neither, but your brain is crying on the inside. Your brain prefers easy tasks, which means short emails that don't create a time suck or additional work. The visual impact of lots of text puts the brain into resistance mode.

The introduction of new information that requires attention forces the brain to make a time/value decision subconsciously. "Do I really want to invest the time in this?" If there's too much, you'll earn a quick delete.

Next time you're on websites like Amazon.com or Zappos.com, pick a product and go to that product's detail page. Choose a book, or a shoe, or a piece of clothing. One thing you'll notice is the way the product descriptions are written. On Zappos.com, you'll see a product description associated with a product, where only a sentence or two are visible, then the paragraph blurs. Underneath that paragraph, you'll see a link to "Read More," which reveals a longer description. When you visit the Amazon.com page for purchasing this book, you'll see only a portion of the product description is visible, then an invitation to "Read More" under the blurred out bottom of the second paragraph.

Why do they do that? Zappos, Amazon, and so many other companies have figured out how to avoid tripping your reptilian brain. Again, that's the part of your brain that makes subconscious, split-second decisions. When the reptilian brain smells information overload, it subconsciously makes the decision to move on. Presenting only a few sentences, versus the entirety of the text, creates a visual for the brain of being less work, and as a result, subconsciously looks more attractive.

In other words, when someone sends you an email which is so text heavy that it resembles the book *War and Peace*, your brain subconsciously perceives the email as an unwanted, interruptive project.

So, think "Twitter" length instead of *War and Peace*. Twitter requires your messages to be under 240 characters, just long enough to educate without inundating. If you can't fit your initial message into 240 characters or less, there's a diminishing return to every character that follows. The average word length in the English language is 5.1 characters,[3] so you're looking at no longer

---

3   http://www.wolframalpha.com/input/?i=average+english+word+length

than 47 words. Can you do it? Of course you can.

One of my favorite sales trainers and prospecting experts is John Barrows. In his blog post called "Content versus Context," he writes, "...if we as sales reps are just blasting out template emails, [sharing] content...without adding any context or insights then we're no different than Marketing...The sales reps who will survive are the ones who will put insightful context around the content to help build their brand and thrive."[4]

Your targets likely no longer want to talk to you if they don't have to, and they certainly won't read any of your "filibuster" email.

RECREATING THE "READ MORE..." IN YOUR PROSPECTING EMAILS

You've engaged your target via a well-framed subject line, a compelling first few words of the email body, which drove them to open the email. You've structured the email in a way that visually is not causing the reader's brain to see it as a lot of extra work to be done, and the content contained in the email matches the content contained in the subject line and first few words of the body. There is no sales pitch, only personalized value. Now what?

As we discussed above, Zappos.com only makes the first few sentences of their product description visible on their product page because it does not want to exhaust the user's brain up front. You can use the same approach in your emails. Your goal is to give the reader an easy path to learn about your products and services without cluttering the email itself.

The simplest way to provide a path for the reader to understand who you and your company are is to include a link to your company in your email signature. The link should be easy to see, find, and click. In the email I received recently

---

4   Barrows, John. "Content Versus Context." *The Make It Happen Blog*, 1 Feb. 2018, jbarrows. com/blog/content-versus-context/

from a company that provided me with a link to an email template I could use when putting together a quarterly board presentation, there was no mention of what this individual's company offers, however, the link to their company's website was clearly visible. I clicked it.

Another more modern way to guide an interested prospect who has engaged with your email to learn more about your company is through email signature technology.

What is email signature technology, you ask?

Your company is on a company-wide email system, I would assume. You probably have an email signature block that populates at the bottom of each email, typically featuring your name, title, and contact information. Email signature technology turns your contact information into an asset.

An email signature technology provider headquartered in Indianapolis, Sigstr, allows organizations to leverage the signature block space on your individual outbound emails, ensuring consistent branding and an opportunity to further engage. Through their ABM (Account Based Marketing) functionality, Sigstr allows you to customize a banner ad along with your email signature.

For example, imagine you work for Sigstr, and you are prospecting to a company called Klowd. You're targeting Klowd's CMO (chief marketing officer). You send a simple, two sentence, personalized and valuable email to her. Then, as shown in this example below, Sigstr created a path to more information via the email banner, coupled with an email signature, that says, "Hi Klowd! Allow us to introduce ourselves!" The recipient can click through if she wishes and appreciates the customization. Then, you can track click-through rates through Sigstr's technology.

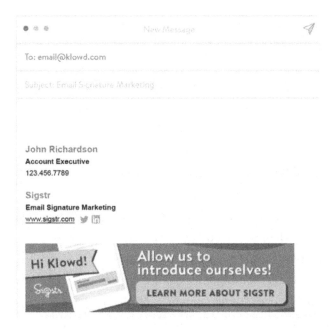

PHOTO: A sample customized email signature provided by Sigstr to the company, Klowd.

Given the volume of emails the recipient likely receives, one that is personalized, adds value, short, and provides a simple path to engage would stand out, wouldn't it?

BE "IN DEMAND"

Imagine you and a friend are walking down the street in a city you've never been. The two of you decide you're hungry and are now looking for a place to eat.

As you look down the street, you see two restaurants you've never heard of before—one on the left side of the street, and one on the right. Both appear to be interesting in terms of their restaurant category. The one on the left side of the street has a couple of people milling about outside of it, and it appears as though you can see people in the window. The one on the right side of the street doesn't look to have much activity going on around it. It appears empty. Which one do you choose?

When I have asked this question to large groups, the overwhelming majority raise their hands when asked if they would choose the restaurant on the left side of the street, the one with more people in it. There's very little logic going on in this decision. The "feeling" is that the restaurant on the left side of the street must be better, because there are lots of people there.

Restaurant owners have started to embrace this concept with amazing results. One person told me about how the owner of their restaurant, which happens to be in a suburban location, no longer has all of their employees park in the back or in remote spots in the parking lot. Instead, a handful of employees park up-front, where the cars are visible. By taking this approach, they are creating the perception that people are inside dining. Second, I met an owner who would stand at the counter appearing to be looking over the menu when there was nobody in line at his restaurant. Again, the goal is in making people feel like they're not alone in their pursuit of your products or services.

In a business setting, if your potential buyers are unfamiliar with you and don't know much about you, as a seller, you must create that feeling that there are patrons in the restaurant (your business). Creating the impression that your business is in-demand will disarm them and call their attention.

Think about how available you make yourself look in your email prospecting efforts. I have cut and pasted the closing line from the last four cold emails I received, plus a bonus fifth email below that. There is no editing here:

1. "Do you have fifteen minutes for a brief intro call over the next few days?"

2. "Todd, what is your availability to discuss Wednesday or Thursday?"

3. "Are you available for a quick phone call sometime in the next few days? Please let me know what days/times work best for you."

4. "When do you have ten minutes to chat in the next week or so?"

And the fifth email? It ends with a request of me. "Please click on the link to my calendar to schedule a time with me." For fun, I clicked the link, which brought me to his "Calendy" page, which is a convenient link to this salesperson's calendar, where I can self-schedule a meeting with him if I so desire.

I arrived at his availability. I clicked three days out. For this account executive, every single time was available for the day with the exception of the lunch hour. So, for fun, I clicked on another day...and again, completely open. He literally had nothing else scheduled. I could have picked any time from 9 a.m.-5 p.m. aside from the lunch hour any day for weeks.

There's a balance in trying to be flexible for your potential buyers, and that is understandable. However, you're creating the impression that you're not in high demand. It screams, "Please accept, because nobody else will talk to me."

Be specific and suggest specific dates and times. **Otherwise, you are the equivalent of the restaurant on the right.** (The empty one!) For example, suggesting a specific date and time like, "How does Wednesday morning at 10 a.m. work for you?" creates a stronger impression of potential demand. Or, provide a couple of options. What is the worst that can happen? The potential buyer isn't available either of those times, and you have to find another time? If you're using a scheduling app, create available time windows. Schedule your day to be as productive as possible, with categories of activities scheduled in batches. That way, you could provide a two-to-three-hour window each day for your potential buyers to schedule times with you, reserving the rest of the day for research, prospecting, follow up calls and emails, or other regular responsibilities vital to your goal attainment. Any suggestion that your calendar is wide open subconsciously sends the wrong message.

PERSONALIZED VALUE LASTS...GIMMICKY TRICKS DON'T

Dr. A.K. Pradeep talks about the concept of "novelty" in his book *The Buying Brain*. He says that novelty is the single most effective factor in capturing the brain's precious attention. Back when we were "hunters," our brains were wired to look for something brilliant and new: something that stood out from the landscape, something that looked delicious. That inherent mechanism still exists in our brain, to where a unique message or product can help penetrate the selective subconscious mind of your buyer.[5]

Novelty is hard to come by when you're on the receiving end of so many emails and phone calls a day. In my role as chief revenue officer, I was constantly cleaning out fifty to one hundred voicemails every couple of weeks. My email inbox was consistently filled with between one hundred to two hundred messages per day, and that's only because I created email filters.

The "history of prospecting" would be an interesting book. When a technique is proven to work, the next thing you know, every prospecting salesperson is using it. Knowing that our brains are wired to resist "influence," once a new technique is determined to be an attempt at influence, your prospects' brains will create new filters to block anyone that attempts to sell to them that way.

When selling, it is important to continually disrupt your customers' brain filters. Recall a time when you were driving down a highway, singing along with whatever song is on the radio or considering the day's news, when suddenly you realized you hadn't been paying any attention to the road for the past few miles. You had been driving at 70+ miles per hour on autopilot, and even your reptilian brain was fine with the "not paying attention" part. Similarly, buyers' brain maps are subconsciously swatting you away when your approach is just like everyone else's...just like the last few miles of farmland you've been driving through.

---

5   A.K. Pradeep, *The Buying Brain* (Hoboken, NJ: John Wiley & Sons, Inc., 2010), 29.

Being different means being creative. Doing something unexpected is creative. When you come across a "trick" or a technique that others are using to get engagements from prospects, be careful. Those tricks are soon wired into the brain's influence filter, and recognized as a gimmicky sales technique.

A style that always has the chance of bypassing a buyer's influence filter is personalization. Don't give the target homework. But instead, give them an easy path to learn more if *they* so choose. One click.

NEGATIVITY BIAS

You're passionate about what you sell, right? Does that come through in your communications?

Email researcher Jocelyn Glei talks about something called the "negativity bias" in email.[6] Here's my take on what she said. Think about the emotion you have when writing an email on a scale from 1-10. If your excitement over what you just sent is a 10, the person on the receiving end won't have that same level of excitement over it...thus, a negativity bias. In prospecting emails, the excitement of your reader will always be lower than the excitement of the writer. So, that reader may, for math's sake, read it and feel a 7. Most emails I read are written at a 5, and so I'm reading it at a 2.

In other words, if your excitement level regarding what you're sending is mediocre, and that level of mediocre energy is flowing through in the words and communication style you use in your email outreach, the perception on the other end will be less-than-mediocre.

The brain is wired to make decisions based on feelings, and then justify those feelings with logic. What feelings are you communicating in your messages?

---

6   Glei, Jocelyn K. "Six Ways To Write Emails That Don't Make People Silently Resent You." Fast Company, Fast Company, 10 Mar. 2017, www.fastcompany.com/3068741/six-ways-to-write-emails-that-dont-make-people-silently-resent-you

Inspiration? Anger? Lust? Think about the words you use. Do they exude feeling?

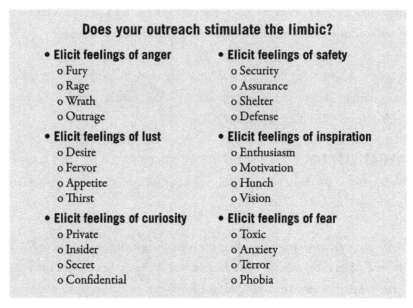

Does your outreach stimulate the limbic?

- **Elicit feelings of anger**
  - Fury
  - Rage
  - Wrath
  - Outrage
- **Elicit feelings of lust**
  - Desire
  - Fervor
  - Appetite
  - Thirst
- **Elicit feelings of curiosity**
  - Private
  - Insider
  - Secret
  - Confidential
- **Elicit feelings of safety**
  - Security
  - Assurance
  - Shelter
  - Defense
- **Elicit feelings of inspiration**
  - Enthusiasm
  - Motivation
  - Hunch
  - Vision
- **Elicit feelings of fear**
  - Toxic
  - Anxiety
  - Terror
  - Phobia

Fig. 5.3 - Examples of words that inspire feeling.

Read through the words in Figure 5.3. Do they make you "feel" something when you read them? Use words that elicit feelings in your communications. Intense feeling words will enhance the impact of the message for the reader.

FINAL THOUGHTS: WHAT ABOUT THE PHONE?

It is hard to refute the argument that telephone prospecting is slowly losing its effectiveness as a prospecting tool. It does and will continue to play a role, but my belief is that the telephone is no longer the preferred means of building a pipeline.

Just like our children are growing up with easy access to the opinions of other consumers for their apps, movies, dates, and products they purchase, they are also growing up with "people-avoiding" technology: text messaging, social media, online chat, and many other paths which allow us to be more efficient with our time. Part of the value of these screen communication paths is that we can perfect our message before sending it out. Because of this, speaking to someone "live" actually creates anxiousness in the brain. Technology is becoming a tool for avoiding stressful situations.

This means that we turn to the actual phone for help less than we did even five years ago. We order our food and groceries online, and Google is testing AI technology that will literally make our phone calls for us.[7] Want to make a restaurant reservation? Picking up the phone to make it is so 2015! We're making our reservations on websites and apps like OpenTable more than ever. Sellers must adjust to the effect that this shift has had on buyers.

The mindset is three-fold:

1. The buyer's brain is resistant to being "sold to" or influenced, which is now the primary assumption of an unrecognized phone call;

2. Managers and executives are considerably more in control of their schedules, desiring not to be driven by interruptions; and

3. For unsolicited or unrecognized calls, managers and executives more often consider the idea that "if it's important, they'll leave a message. If it isn't important, they're wasting my time."

To have the highest impact, it is my belief that we should all be focused on maximizing our effectiveness on the channels that buyers prefer to communicate with today. Do not abandon the phone. It still is a necessary prospecting mechanism, but the best practices that are taught in countless other channels are the ways to go.

---

7   Vincent, James. "Google's AI Sounds like a Human on the Phone - Should We Be Worried?" The Verge, 9 May 2018, www.theverge.com/2018/5/9/17334658/google-ai-phone-call-assistant-duplex-ethical-social-implications

KEEPERS

Prospecting is the beginning of relationship development with a potential buyer. To develop a strong relationship:

- **Always be giving**: Focus your efforts on *giving* without an expectation or request of reciprocation from your targets.
- **Optimize your subject line plus ten**: Ensure that your intentions are reflected in the subject line plus the first ten words of the email body.
- **Deliver succinct, personalized value**: If you're leading with "I" or "we" you are white noise to the executive inbox. Your emails must reflect personalization and contain value to have impact.
- **Be in-demand**: While you might assume that always being available might be considered valuable for your prospects, the buying brain subconsciously prefers that you create the impression that you and your company are "in demand."

CHAPTER SIX

POSITIONING

"To know that you do not know is the best.
To pretend to know when you do not know is a disease."

—Lao-Tzu

AVE YOU EVER BEEN TO AN IKEA STORE? IF YOU HAVEN'T, YOU'RE probably aware of who they are. IKEA, represented by its massive buildings of blue and yellow, is a furniture retailer founded in Sweden, selling what's called "modernist," Scandinavian-designed pieces and accessories for practically every room in the house.

When you visit an IKEA, the process by which you select a piece of furniture is unorthodox. For example, imagine you're in the market for a new bed for a child's room. First, you'll wander the floors of the store trying to figure out where the bed frames are located, and specifically the children's bed frames. There are arrows on the ground that wind you through the store in a serpentine fashion. The smell of food permeates the massive store floors, as they have a restaurant offering many Swedish staples, the best of which (in my opinion) are the meatballs.

Upon arriving at the children's room section, you browse the many pieces and set ups, with uncommon brand names like SLÄKT and SVÄRTA.

Upon selecting the bed frame you like, the next step is to figure out how to actually purchase your selection. On the displayed bed frame you'll find a tag containing some basic product information, the price of the pieces including a total when they're all purchased together, and product codes to help you locate the items in their warehouse. Yes...to help YOU locate the items YOURSELF. You can either write down all of the numbers or grab your phone and take a picture of the tag.

If you thought that was fun, you now make your way through the maze of showrooms until you arrive back at the escalators, then head down to the first-floor warehouse.

If you're looking for a fun distraction, sit at the top of the escalators and watch as customers who have opted to use a shopping cart struggle to fit it in into the dedicated "shopping cart" escalator. While it seems fairly simple, at least one out of five users will experience some sort of catastrophe. You'll thank me!

Next, you grab a wheeled cart, which seems to have been designed for an *America's Funniest Home Videos* show instead of the transport of furniture. You traverse the massive warehouse and look for your item's aisle number, then the specific slot where the piece is located. Upon matching your desired bed frame's item number from the picture on your phone to one of the many boxes, you begin the process of pulling the large, heavy box from the slot onto the wheeled cart. Did I mention that the wheels on the cart don't lock? So, as you're attempting to load the two-ton boxes onto the cart, odds are the cart has decided to roll away.

For any complex piece of furniture like a children's bed frame, it's likely the frame itself will be in one aisle, while the bed slats will be located in another. The process of wheeling the cart through a maze of people while the wheels refuse to cooperate continues until you've found all of your pieces and are now fully loaded. It's finally time to roll your way to the checkout aisles, then off to the parking lot.

Oh, the parking lot! You're not allowed to wheel your furniture purchase all the way out to your car. There's a good reason for this rule, as I can't imagine what it would be like to have people rolling massive carts out to their cars, attempting to pack their cars while other cars and people are departing or arriving. So, you are required to leave the furniture pieces behind a steel barred area, drive your car to the designated loading area, back it in, and then load it.

You begin the drive home exhausted, and likely with the souvenir of a minor, lingering injury or two to make the experience even more memorable.

All of this with almost zero assistance from any IKEA employee.

Upon arriving home, you drag the boxes into your home, open them up, and find that your nightmare has only just begun.

There, in the box, sits 100+ unlabeled pieces waiting to be assembled by you, and instructions that often do not contain a single word. Only drawings. Enjoying low-level gambling myself, my wife likes to set an "over/under" on the number of f-bombs I will explode over the course of the assembly experience.

If you were IKEA's competitor, wouldn't you think it would be incredibly easy to create a better experience for your shopper? The experience is inefficient, inconvenient, and downright painful in many cases. Well, guess what? IKEA continues to be the largest furniture retailer in the world, with 415 stores across 49 different countries.[1]

IKEA doesn't hide their flaws. Customers expect to have this experience when they go to the store, and as a result, the experience is less unpleasant.

Your memory of the event might go something like this: "Remember last time we went to IKEA? I still have a scar from trying to load that couch into my

---

1   "IKEA," Wikipedia, https://en.wikipedia.org/wiki/IKEA (accessed Sept. 12, 2018).

hatchback. That was awful." But you'll end the story with this: "Anyway, I'm thinking about adding a cabinet. Want to go on Saturday?"

IKEA has created a highly profitable business model that provides stylish furniture at very reasonable prices, and has generated notable customer loyalty. IKEA wears their flaws instead of hiding them. They essentially tell the world, "Here's what we don't do, but if you're okay with that, here's what you're going to love."

Similarly, Progressive Insurance will give you a quote for your insurance needs, however, they'll also provide you with the rates of their three nearest competitors.[2] The concept is a brilliant use of transparency. They know that it is likely that the customer will call their competitors, so why not save them the time? For Progressive, this is a "win even if they lose" approach. They've established themselves as the transparent insurance company, and they recognize that even if their price is slightly higher than a competitor's, you're likely to stay given the sunk cost of time; you have already gone through the process of providing your information in order to secure a new policy. Going to another company would essentially require that you start over. Progressive has grown to become the fourth largest consumer insurance company in the United States.[3]

The truth is, no matter what you sell, it probably isn't perfect. If you're selling technology, it will have flaws. If you're selling real estate, the home you're selling could be next door to a crazy neighbor, or maybe there will be ants in the pantry. If you're in the recruiting space, almost every candidate has a flaw on their resume. Don't be afraid of the flaws in your offerings, as exposing those flaws may be the very reason your customers engage with you, buy from you, and keep buying from you.

---

2   "Progressive Auto Insurance - An Introduction." Progressive, www.progressive.com/about/history/

3   Hanley, Ryan. "Do The 10 Biggest Car Insurance Companies Give You the Best Service?" TrustedChoice.com, Sept. 2016, www.trustedchoice.com/f/p/largest-auto-insurance-companies/

APPLYING TRANSPARENCY IN SELLING

Late in 2017, a major apparel brand in New York was kicking off an evaluation to determine which ratings and reviews technology to use on their website.

The contact from this apparel brand, Derek, told Greg, the sales representative assigned to the account, that he would like to meet with our team in the coming weeks to get a better idea of our place in the market, discuss initial pricing, and kick off a formal evaluation.

Greg told his manager about this potential opportunity to work with this well-known brand, who texted me to tell me the good news.

As it turned out, I was in New York when I received the text. I suggested that Greg reach back out to Derek, tell him that I was in town right now, and suggest a quick coffee meeting. Greg reached out, and Derek took us up on the offer, inviting me to his office that afternoon.

Upon arriving at Derek's office, the design certainly reflected the brand. I was sent up to the fourth floor in their Manhattan office. As the elevator doors opened, a disturbing life-size picture of a young boy in just his underwear greeted me in the elevator area. I was quite taken aback. Apparently this brand wasn't afraid to be transparent.

Derek met me at the elevator, and we made our way back to his office. He was all business, reflecting a "New York" approach to dealing with potential vendors, which I would classify as direct and efficient.

Upon arriving in his office, which was small given it was in downtown Manhattan, a group of people were collecting chairs to pack people into a room in anticipation of my presentation. While the office couldn't have been more than 10' x 12', Derek managed to squeeze eight of his team members into the room. While I hadn't quite prepared for such an expansive meeting, I plugged my laptop into Derek's 21" monitor in case I had to show them something on it.

Derek started the meeting with a directive. "Todd, your competitor was in late last week. They pitched us on their offering and were pretty impressive. However, we wanted to talk to you, too, as from our research, it appears as though you may be a viable option."

He continued, "So, to cut through the crap, can you start by explaining the differences between you and them, and what we can expect to be better about your company?"

I replied, "Sure. I'd be happy to. However, would it be helpful if I start with how they're better than us? There are a couple of things they do that we don't... and, as a matter of fact, those items aren't even on our product roadmap in terms of priorities for the future. Much of what our two companies provide is very similar, however, if the true differentiators are vital requirements for you, given that so many employees are investing their time in being here, we could decide to end the meeting early."

You could sense Derek's demeanor immediately change. It was as though he exhaled and dropped his guarded wall. While he was clearly trying to own the room and show who was boss when I walked in, he was now smiling and welcoming.

"Oh, that would be great. Please do!"

I went on to explain how our competitor had taken their product development roadmap in a direction that wasn't a match to ours. I explained the value of the differentiated offering our competitor provides, and how some of this competitor's clients were leveraging it.

Once I finished this short explanation, Derek looked around the small office, and it was clear his team didn't feel strongly about our competitor's value-added differentiator. Derek thanked me for the candor, and communicated that those differentiators weren't important, and that if they became important in the future, he knew enough about them to know that other companies offered that sort of functionality which could easily "plug in" to our offering.

The rest of the discussion was magic. Similar to how IKEA tells the world what they don't offer so they can be great at the things they do, I talked about why we had chosen the direction and focus reflected in our offering and roadmap. I talked about our differentiators, and why their specific organization should care about them. I also sprinkled some reminders regarding how we ensure smooth implementation (to reduce perceived complexity), and what kinds of things they should expect to encounter once they became a customer.

With about fifteen minutes left in the allotted time, Derek kicked everyone out of his office except for me. He was incredibly engaged, and warmed up to me at this point in the discussion. He grabbed a red folder from a rack on his desk, pulling out what looked like a balance sheet from the file. He pointed to a line item on the financial document that said "Ratings and Reviews," with a number next to it.

"Todd, how do we get our investment to match or beat this number?"

While our average sales cycle length is anywhere from four to six months with a company of this type, Derek signed the contract within four weeks of this meeting.

Leading with our cards played face-up did the following:

1. **It disarmed Derek**: His brain, like all brains, was wired to resist being sold to. Once he knew I wasn't there to sell to him and his team and that I was taking their time and interests into account, his energy and attitude transformed.

2. **It established trust**: Because expectations were set from the first conversation, the negotiation process was easier. Terms in the contract were met with an assumption of good intentions and shared ethical standards.

3. **The competitors were put at a massive disadvantage**: When Derek told our competitor about his decision to go with us, that competitor shared a couple of other issues clients have had in working with us. Derek's response to them was, "Yes, I know. [Todd] told us!"

4. **The sales cycle sped up dramatically**: They didn't have to go through a review process to find out what issues they were going to run into. We told them. When clients have to search for answers they can't get from you, they often don't come back! We controlled the information flow by sharing everything above board, and the purchase cycle was cut down by 75%.

5. **It reduced reference dependency**: While Derek's team did talk to peers at other companies in the course of buying, those peers didn't share anything they hadn't already heard directly from us. As a result, Derek's team did not feel the need to request references, feeling as though they had the information they needed to make a decision, as those outside conversations with his peers actually solidified their trust in us.

6. **It properly set expectations**: We earned the "benefit of the doubt" in the post-sale process when any inevitable problems occurred post sale. Their perception of the onboarding experience was more positive overall.

Here's how to do it:

Step 1: As we discussed in Chapter 2, figure out where your buyers go if they are looking for independent information on your pros and cons.

Step 2: Do your homework to understand exactly what both you offer and your competitors offer. Create a chart. How do your competitors position their unique offerings?

Step 3: Match your competitors' unique offerings up against your understanding of your client's requirements. Which differences matter? Which flaws will matter?

Step 4: Put them in order, from what you perceive to be least important to most important to the buyer.

Step 5: Pick a couple of those offerings from the top of the list, and communicate those to the client. "To ensure we're making the best use of our time together, would it make sense to highlight a couple of the things we DON'T do? If you and your team have determined these to be vitally important to the success of your project, it's likely better to start with those, versus discover them later, right?"

Similarly to the customers IKEA, Progressive, or countless other organizations who have mastered the art of embracing their vulnerabilities, your buyers will appreciate the costs of getting the really important stuff right. Their resistance to influence will fade, their trust in you will blossom, and you'll quickly hone in on what's truly important to the buyer.

POSITIONING AN UPSELL

For many organizations, current customers are the best paths to additional sales. Selling more to an existing client is what is called an "upsell." In the world of B2B sales, those upsell opportunities often come in the form of new product offerings. So often, when describing the features of a new product offering, or when you have an opportunity for an upsell, we have all been taught to lead with the logic. We have all been taught to discuss the incredible, amazing features and benefits this additional product will add to the buyer's experience.

In the ratings and reviews space with PowerReviews, one such offering we would position for our clients is the concept of "sampling." If you were in the consumer products industry, for example, and brought a new offering to the market, you might work with a company like ours to distribute one hundred or so free samples out to the market in exchange for their feedback in the form of a review. Obtaining broad feedback before launching a new product is incredibly valuable to the company internally, and having ratings and reviews available on the product's website from day one aids in conversion (sales) and customer satisfaction.

Sounds great, eh? All sunshine and cotton candy.

However, I liked to take a different approach when presenting this new capability to potential clients. I started with a story about how we screwed up a sampling campaign as we were rolling out the new capability, which ended up disarming the audience of buyers:

"In one instance, we were doing a sampling campaign for a recreational equipment company who was launching a new backyard trampoline. We engaged our database of potential individuals who would want to receive a free trampoline in exchange for providing feedback, and quickly found one hundred takers.

"What we didn't do is make sure that those one hundred people met the require-ments needed for a backyard trampoline. The key word was 'backyard,' as we didn't ask whether they had one. Unfortunately, around forty of the recipients lived in a condominium."

That got a big laugh, and exposing our imperfections served as a huge disarming mechanism for the prospect. We were willing to admit that we aren't perfect and that we've learned valuable lessons from this new "sampling" offering. If you have a new product offering, there are certainly times when it hasn't gone well. There are certainly lessons that have been learned. And, in many cases, they could be really funny, disarming stories that drive the trust factor in your budding relationship in the right direction. Find those stories. Work with your marketing team, your product team, or your client success team to learn about the issues some clients have faced in the past, and what your organization has learned and implemented as a result.

THE ROLE OF YOUR ORGANIZATION

Embrace feedback. If your organization has a list of their core values, add this one. Across your organization, it is now vital to have an always-on radar for what your customers are saying about you, what your competitors are saying about you, what analysts and bloggers are saying about you, and what current and former employees are saying about you.

Senior Leadership: As a part of your senior leadership team's regular meet-ings, I would suggest that you include one regular agenda item that is focused on customer feedback. Consider the CEO of Instant Pot, Robert Wang, who invented the greatest kitchen gadget you never knew you needed through com-bining the functionality of a pressure cooker and a slow cooker in one device. He attributes his company's success to the fact that he and his team have read every single review on their product.[4] And, given the cult following of the Instant Pot, there are now over 39,000 reviews. He uses the feedback in every aspect of his business, from positioning to product development to customer service. In the business-to-business space, your job will be much less daunting to find and curate feedback, as you're unlikely to have 39,000 reviews to read.

Create mechanisms for your employees to share both internal and external feedback. Some ideas include:

- Create an internal Slack channel for employees to submit feedback they see and hear in the market;
- Create a simple form where employees can submit things they've read and heard, available on your Intranet or wherever employees can easily find and access the link; and
- Create an email alias that distributes feedback to your senior leadership team (and/or other teams within your organization who have a need to know), because supporting your organization's efforts through transparency starts at the senior level.

Marketing: Holistically, your marketing team will need to be constantly aware of the chatter about your organization. What are our customers, prospects, potential investors, and competitors saying about our products and services? Marketing will then need to own the messaging and positioning of that feedback. The goal isn't to create a list of reasons why you're inferior, then have a sales organization list them off in an excruciating "This is why we suck" diatribe. The goal is to employ messaging that presents your solutions on the 4.2-4.5 range, not a perfect 5.0.

---

4   Montag, Ali. "On Prime Day, the Instant Pot Sells out and Breaks a New Sales Record in 19 Hours." CNBC, 17 July 2018, www.cnbc.com/2018/07/17/instant-pot-sells-out-and-breaks-new-sales-records.html

Sales Enablement: The sales enablement team will need to turn marketing's messaging into training where sales professionals can practice delivering less than perfect positioning. Take the positioning from marketing, orchestrate the training, and measure the impact.

Everyone else in your organization: Everyone working across your organization—from human resources and finance across to office management and product development—is aware of what the general sentiment in the office is. Seek opportunities to collect and communicate feedback across the organization. Did an employee read something on some obscure website online? Did they hear people talking about your products inadvertently while riding the train in during their commute? In my opinion, giving senior leadership exposure to any type of feedback is valuable. One-off comments from a crazy person you hear on the street may seem inconsequential, but if those comments are centrally collected, it becomes considerably easier to recognize sentiment if those comments turn into a trend.

The negative reviews will not always be fun to hear. But that's ok. The goal is to collect the feedback that is relevant to the buyer, or which the buyer will find on their own while they are evaluating your services. The goal is for there to be no surprises.

KEEPERS

In this chapter, the most important takeaway is the requirement for you and your company to embrace vulnerability in that it gives you power, it doesn't take it away.

- **Lead with your shortcomings:** Your buyer's brain is preparing for a sales pitch. To maximize the impact of your 4.2-4.5 positioning, disarming their sales filter from the beginning by leading with potential showstoppers versus waiting to address them later in the sales cycle will speed sales cycles, speed qualification (or disqualification), speed trust building, and put your competitors at a disadvantage.

- **Transparency as a culture**: Organizations that make collecting feedback and leading with transparency a core company value will be the victors as the ease with which buyers can find feedback grows.

CHAPTER SEVEN

MUTUAL DECISION PLANS

W HEN I WAS A KID, TOYS "R" US WAS THE GREATEST STORE ON Earth. Aisles and aisles, floor to warehouse ceiling, filled with every toy a child could ever want. I remember walking in, adrenaline flowing, running up and down the aisles, eyes bright with anticipation that the rest of my life would now be complete because of the toy I was about to get.

As I write this, Toys "R" Us has filed for bankruptcy, and is in the midst of liquidating its assets and selling everything, including their brick and mortar real estate, at deep discounts.

As such, I made the mistake of bringing my kids to a store in suburban Chicago to try to take advantage of those discounts and witnessed why they're in such trouble, and how that applies to selling.

My kids, who were five and seven years old when we arrived, could have potentially been six and eight by the time decisions were made and we exited the store. As I had experienced as a child, they were overflowing with excitement as we walked through the parking lot, entering the front doors. Minutes later, that anticipation turned to stress, and then downright fatigue for both. Tears were right on the cusp of their eyes, as the process of deciding what toy would change their life had became unexpectedly difficult.

My kids found something that they wanted in just about every aisle within the dollar limit my wife and I outlined. The fear of missing out was crushing them, as they walked aisle to aisle finding another desired toy, then another, then another.

Frustrated ourselves, my wife pulled three of the toys they had indicated they were interested in for each of them and told them they had to decide between the three. The choice was made, albeit with significant consternation, and we then got in line to check out (which was a goat rodeo). While in line, both of our children were in a constant state of second guessing themselves, and the car ride home with the toys of their choosing wasn't filled with joy, but instead with furrowed brows and borderline exhaustion.

What happened? Why is Toys "R" Us nearing the end of its existence, when it's every child's dream store?

While you might think that adding more choices to a shopping experience is valuable, study after study shows that the more choices and decisions you force on the buyer, the more fatigue it causes the brain. As a matter of fact, Roy F. Baumeister, who authored the book *Willpower*, coined the term "decision fatigue." Choices require energy from the brain. As the brain is forced to make decisions, the more fatigued the brain becomes. The more fatigued the brain, the less the brain wants to make future decisions. Limiting choices and decisions is the easier path to a fruitful journey.[1] It is said that Steve Jobs, co-founder of Apple, wore the same clothes every day in order to reduce the number of decisions he would have to make each day.[2]

---

1   http://www-personal.umich.edu/~prestos/Consumption/pdfs/Baumeister-VohsTice2007.pdf

2   Worley, William. "This Is Why Geniuses Always Wear the Same Outfit..." CNN, 9 Oct. 2015, www.cnn.com/2015/10/09/world/gallery/decision-fatigue-same-clothes/index.html

Where does this apply in the sales process, or in any situation where you're seeking to influence someone into a decision? Well, everywhere.

As a selling professional, a buyer seeks out your guidance as the expert. While the buyer is likely the expert on their own organization's needs and processes, you bring information they don't have access to: the experience, expertise, potential pitfalls, and lessons learned from working with many more companies who have similar challenges.

Commonly called either a "Sequence of Events" doc (SoE), or a "Mutual Action Plan" doc (MAP), these documents are designed to lay out the decision-making journey with a buyer. I like to call it a "Mutual Decision Plan" (MDP), which is an incredibly important element of the Transparency Sale, or really any sale. If you do four things, you make decision making so darn easy:

1) **Introduce the MDP early**: A mutual decision plan shows the buyer that you've done this before (which instills confidence, an important "feeling" in making decisions), while also minimizing the decisions the buyer needs to make along the journey.

2) **Make every interaction transparent**: Match the MDP up with transparent selling during every stage of the cycle, which also minimizes the energy the brain requires to resist being "sold to."

3) **Revisit / follow the MDP through the entire process**: Following the plan you've built mutually with the buyer keeps the buyer subconsciously continuing to make "yes" decisions along the journey.

4) **Limit options**: In the end, the brain won't be exhausted from the process, trust is built, and you are making a recommendation versus providing options, which means that decision making happens quickly.

WHAT DOES THE MUTUAL DECISION PLAN (MDP) LOOK LIKE, AND HOW CAN YOU USE IT?

Buyers understand that every purchasing process is different, and usually includes twists, turns, and unexpected surprises. As we've discussed in previous chapters, in most organizations, the decision-making process can be complex, and requires that the buyer has done their homework in making a logical sale based on data and facts, not just feelings.

Creating mutual decision plans provides so much value to both you and the buyer, but many sales professionals feel as though they are being too aggressive in holding a buyer to a specific plan. Instead, they opt for being like a dog chasing a car down the street, having no idea where the car is going. That doesn't work.

It is important to remember that with every interaction, you're either building trust or eroding it. Using an MDP builds confidence that this isn't your or your company's first experience addressing the issues that will arise during the purchasing process.

This isn't a list of things *you* have to do; it's a mutual to-do list for both you and your buyer.

To start, outline the tasks that take place typically in a buying journey, both on your end and your buyer's end. In this example, "Initech" is the buyer, and "Acme" is you, the seller:

Owner	What	When
Acme, Initech	Initial alignment meeting	Today
Initech	Distribution of RFP	November 30th
Acme	Due date for RFP response	December 21st
Initech	Notification of intent to continue	January 5th
Acme, Initech	On-site presentation to Initech team	January 12th-26th
Acme, Initech	Pre-implementation review / scoping	February 2nd
Acme, Initech	Finalize & review details of proposal	February 5th
Initech	Notification of decision	February 15th
Initech	Legal review, redline of legal agreement	March 1st
Acme, Initech	Collaborative agreement on Ts & Cs	March 8th
Acme	Routing for agreement execution	March 15th
Initech	Implementation team officially assigned	March 16th
Acme, Initech	Official kickoff call	March 17th
Acme, Initech	Rollout / implementation	March 17th - April 5th
Acme, Initech	Post go-live metrics review	April 6th
Acme, Initech	Ongoing bi-weekly business review	Begins April 13th

Fig. 7.1. An example of a mutual to-do list for a buyer (Initech) and a seller (Acme).

There's a lot here, but in a complex sale, these steps are likely required for the buyer to make a purchase and realize their expected business impact. Drop it into a collaborative doc (like a Google Sheet) and review it with the buyer. Ask questions like: "Is there anything missing that you're going to need to do?" "Are any of these steps unnecessary in your decision journey?" "What elements will take longer than the time period I've proposed?" "Which elements will need to be accelerated?" "Who, other than yourself, needs to be involved in this?" "Do we need to include steps to ensure they're aligned?"

Once you've collaborated on the plan, some amazing things happen:

1. **A Truly Qualified Opportunity**: There can be no doubt you have an engaged, qualified opportunity. They're vested through their engagement and involvement in configuring and agreeing to the MDP.

2. **A Confident Buyer**: You've instilled a great deal of confidence in your buyer that you are taking them on a journey you've been on before. Risk is a fire inside a buyer's brain. By using the plan, you're throwing water on that fire. Just like a doctor performing surgery, if they don't share a plan with you, and simply say, "Well, we'll see how this goes. I'm going to do the surgery, we'll see how you're doing and what you need, then we'll determine the next steps," you would freak out.

3. **An Early Warning System**: The MDP becomes an active document that keeps your buyer on track. These items can be put on a calendar now. They become priorities, versus an "I'll call you next week and we'll determine the next steps." Obstacles are transparent from the beginning. These steps, while there are a bunch, are very doable.

If the buying journey looks easy and is easy, then trust is built. None of the steps above look like horrifyingly painful steps. Keep it simple.

I can't help but picture a toy store who has spent the time to get to know your child. When your child walks into the store, a map is provided to the child showing them the path to evaluate what should be their top two or three choices, the process to make the decision, and checkpoints to ensure they stay on track. In the end, the decision should be easy to make. When the brain isn't exhausted from the journey, decisions get made.

KEEPERS

Your buyers need your help to navigate the complexities of a high consideration purchase.

- **Be their Sherpa**: Create a map for their buying purchase, and mutually configure it with the client. While it may feel like an imposition, your best-qualified opportunities will appreciate your efforts to reduce the decision-making burden.

SECTION 3:

WHY YOU?

CHAPTER EIGHT

PRESENTING

"Let's see what happens when you're driving with the 'other guy's' brake pads.
You're drivin' along, you're drivin' along, the kids start shouting from the
back seat, 'I gotta go to the bathroom, Daddy!' 'Not now, damn it!'
Truck tire. EEEEEEEE! I CAN'T STOP! There's a cliff! AAAAAHH!
And your family's screaming, 'Oh my God, we're burning alive!'
'No! I can't feel my legs!' "
–Tommy Callahan (Chris Farley) in the movie *Tommy Boy*

HAVING A DEFINED SALES PROCESS IS A GIVEN IN MOST ORGANIZA-
tions today. Per our discussion in Chapter 4, while many of these sales
processes are rightfully designed to recognize buyer behaviors, they serve
as a foundational framework to ensure efficiency, consistency, and a guide
to the buying journey.

However, what I've rarely found is an organization who has implemented a
presentation process. While many organizations have their "standard deck,"
the need to have a "framework" from which sales teams can configure a cus-
tomer-focused presentation that's consistent, efficient, and tells a great story
has become more important, given what we've learned about how the brain
engages, listens, and learns.

A few years ago, I had just taken over as the SVP of sales for a startup technology company in Chicago. We were just finding ourselves, learning how to work with each other, and scaling up as quickly as we could. Nobody was "ramped" yet, in that none of us felt like we had a repeatable process, a full grasp of what we were positioning, or whether this machine-of-a-business we were building would even work.

One morning soon into our launch and my tenure, a large, multinational Fortune 500 appliance manufacturer appeared on our inbound lead queue. For the purpose of this story, let's call them Whirlsung Corporation.

The lead notification from Whirlsung read, "We're using [Competitor] today and are interested in learning about what your solution can provide." Whirlsung wasn't just using the competitor's solution; our competitor had just named them their "Customer of the Year" at their annual user conference.

Our CEO was the first to see the lead, noticing the email on his mobile phone as he was leaving the office for the day, having just arrived down the elevator from our office on the fifth floor. He was so excited about the opportunity to get in front of Whirlsung, he ran up the stairs back into the office, chomping at the bit to get involved.

We quickly assembled a team that included him, our CTO, our CCO (chief customer officer), an enterprise account executive to quarterback the process, and myself. After completing a brief discovery call, our CEO offered up a visit, where we would take the short drive to their office and tell Whirlsung about what we do. They obliged and scheduled ninety minutes for us.

The team put together the first draft of the "deck" – the collection of slides that would be presented during the meeting. With Slide #1 being the cover, here were the next few in the first draft:

- Slide 2: The Agenda - which listed out the topics we were going to discuss. Primarily about us.
- Slide 3: Our Company Bio - with our logo prominently shown, it bulleted out when we were founded, who our backers/investors were, how many employees we had, and our mission statement.
- Slide 4: A Map - which showed our headquarters office in Chicago, then a dot over in San Francisco, and another in London, as we had a small office already established in Europe.
- Slide 5: A "Nascar" Slide - called that because it looks like a racing stock car, covered in logos. This slide showed the logos of all of the initial clients we were working with.
- Slide 6: Our Products - in beautiful bubbles, this slide listed out all of the products we had encompassed by a larger circle with the name of our "solution."

The first section of the presentation was designed as all "us" and no "them." The configuration of this first draft of the presentation to be given to Whirlsung wasn't wrong or unintelligent. As a matter of fact, almost every presentation I had ever seen was structured that exact same way. In all the brain research, I made a discovery. There's a way to choreograph a presentation that not only engages your audience throughout, but also compels an audience to action.

Let's start with the brain science considerations which will be important for your presentation development.

EMPATHY FOR THE LISTENER

As we were approaching the offices of Whirlsung, we tried to imagine what was going on in their world.

We can guess that, in their brains, there's a voice saying, "Ugh. In fifteen minutes I have to stop what I'm doing, head down to the windowless conference room, and spend the following hour-and-a-half being sold to. I sure hope they have the cure to what ails me."

When those fifteen minutes are up, they make their walk down the hallway into the conference room, where you're there getting set up. Each attendee is bringing their problems with them. Often, they are thinking about what else they could be using this upcoming time slot for, whether it's the problem they just left at their desk, or the pile of emails in their inbox. You're up against that. You'd better make this good.

And even deeper than that, your attendee's brain isn't wired to want to pay attention anyway.

Our brain's number one priority is to get its genes to the next generation...so, survival and reproduction. Your presentation is pretty low on your audience's brain's priority list. The reptilian brain, subconsciously, is always first in a state of wanting to make sure it's not going to get killed during the presentation. Then it wants to make sure there's enough to eat around.[1] The listener, during a presentation, is in a constant state of overriding their reptilian brain distractions. It's your role to make that process of paying attention and absorbing information easier.

Something else to keep in mind when walking into a selling situation: You are about to walk in, smile, make some small talk, and attempt to be disarming. However "nice" you are, the attendee's brain is looking out for signs that you are going to try to influence them. In a way, you are a threat to the audience.

Knowing that our audience needs help maintaining attention during a presentation, and the beginning of your presentation will define their perspective on whether you're there to influence them, the choreography of our presentation is important to get right. Your choreography will need to tell a great story, and compel the listener to action.

---

1   Michael Gazzaniga, *Who's In Charge* (New York: HarperCollins, 2011), 69.

THE ROLE OF EMOTION AND FEAR IN PERSUASION

Many years ago, my team and I were presenting at a Fortune 100 manufacturing company to a room full of executives. I was part of a team that was selling to this company, and reported to our global account manager named Tom, who was our lead presenter. As Tom was presenting, one of the company's executives, who happened to be their vice president of manufacturing, fell asleep. I had the pleasure of sitting next to this gentleman. Not only was he asleep, but he was snoring. Not only was he snoring, but he was writing on his notepad. Not only was he writing on his notepad, but he wrote the word "fear." Turns out he had narcolepsy, and this was a normal occurrence according to his peers. But the fact that he wrote the word "fear" while unconscious, snoring, and listening to the presentation will forever be etched in my memory.

EMOTION BINDS US

Selling to a group versus an individual is especially hard, given that these individuals all come to a purchase evaluation with unique personal beliefs, motivations, fears, hopes, and desires. When attempting to influence individuals who may have a preconceived opinion before walking into the room for your presentation, the approach you take can have unintended consequences.

In psychology, the term "the boomerang effect"refers to what happens during an attempt to persuade someone, but end up solidifying their opposing position instead.[2] In simple terms, this means that when we present people with logical information and data that conflicts with their previously held beliefs, the individuals often will work to configure counterarguments to the presented data, making their original belief stronger in their own mind. This is also often referred to as "confirmation bias," which describes how we naturally and subconsciously hear and interpret facts to confirm what we already believe.[3]

---

2   Boomerang Effect." Wikipedia, 20 Dec. 2015, en.wikipedia.org/wiki/Boomerang_effect

3   Cherry, Kendra. "Why Do We Favor Information That Confirms Our Existing Beliefs?" Verywell Mind, Sept. 2018, www.verywellmind.com/what-is-a-confirmation-bias-2795024

When presenting to a group, we have already discussed how the role of feelings and emotion drives decisions, but it does something else, too. It's been shown to bring an audience's brain in synch. A presentation rich in emotion is a much stronger path than one rich in data and logic to bringing a group of people together. A number of studies have been done to prove this concept works. In one such study, participants were connected to an MRI scanner, and had their brain activity recorded while watching the old Clint Eastwood movie, *The Good, the Bad and the Ugly*.[4] The brain activity among the participants was strangely similar while they watched the movie. Telling a story is a connector. However, the study revealed that the participants' brains synched almost exactly during the moments of the movie which were the most emotional.

In another example, following the terrorist attacks on our country that took place on September 11, 2001, President George W. Bush's approval rating was over 90%.[5] That was the highest approval rating ever recorded for a president. After such a traumatic experience as September 11, emotion brought the entire country together, regardless of political beliefs.

When we present information logically, we may be subconsciously causing a group to solidify opposing views to a potential purchase. When we present stories and emotion, then support that emotion with logic, the result is a much higher propensity to drive connectedness and consensus.

FEAR IS IRRATIONAL AND CAN DISTANCE YOUR BUYER FROM YOU

So, how do we create an emotionally-binding experience in a selling presentation? Focusing on fear is less effective than focusing on a reward.

4   Malach, Rafael. "A Rose By Any Other Name." Weizmann Wonder Wander, 11 Sept. 2016, wis-wander.weizmann.ac.il/life-sciences/rose-any-other-name

5   Gallup, Inc. "Presidential Approval Ratings -- Gallup Historical Statistics and Trends." Gallup.com, news.gallup.com/poll/116677/presidential-approval-ratings-gallup-histo-ri-cal-statistics-trends.aspx

Fear is inconsistent and irrational. For example, consider the top five leading causes of death: heart disease, cancer, chronic lower respiratory disease, accidents, and strokes.[6] Do they match the top five most common fears held by adults? Not at all. The top five phobias are the fears of spiders (arachnophobia), snakes (ophidiophobia), heights (acrophobia), open or crowded spaces (agoraphobia), and surprisingly, dogs (cynophobia).[7] Why aren't our greatest fears aligned with the actual greatest threats we face?

Focusing on short-term rewards is a more effective mechanism than attempting to gain consensus through a set of long-term fears which may never become actual threats. A short-term "carrot" has a greater impact than a longer term "stick." In a presentation, you theoretically want to create a pull towards your solution. Our brains are wired to move towards a reward, and away from a threat. For example, if I were to lay a stack of $100 bills in front of you, you would move towards those bills. If I were to replace those $100 bills with a rattlesnake, your instinct would be to move away.

During your presentations, bringing your audience in through messages of short-term reward, while subconscious, will have greater results than instinctually moving them away.

To bring these concepts together––focusing your presentation on the client, empathizing with their state of mind and attention span during a presentation, emphasizing emotion over data, and emphasizing rewards over fear––let's now focus on how to choreograph your presentation.

---

6   https://www.medicalnewstoday.com/articles/282929.php

7   Olesen, Jacob. "Top 10 Phobias of All Time – 2018 Update." FearOf.net, 13 July 2018, www.fearof.net/top-10-phobias-of-all-time/.

EXTREME MAKEOVER, CLIENT EDITION

The brain represents only about 3% of our body weight but uses 20% of our energy.[8] In other words, it's an energy hog. As a result, delivering a message that is easy to process is something the brain very much enjoys. Easy comes in many forms, and one of them is telling a great story.

I discovered something fascinating as I fed my addiction to reality television makeover shows. "Reality TV" has been a genre of TV shows all the way back to 1973 when the show *An American Family* debuted. In 1992, MTV launched a show called *The Real World* that spawned many copycats. One specific genre within the reality TV world is that of "reality makeover" shows.

The "reality makeover" genre includes shows like *The Biggest Loser*, a weight loss show that works with individuals who have a lot weight to lose, and *Restaurant Impossible*, which takes over a struggling restaurant and turns it around in 48 hours, as well as over 130 other reality television shows focused on taking an unfortunate situation, and turning it completely around in no time at all.

The amazing thing I discovered while watching these shows was the connection between how the shows were choreographed, and what they had in common with great sales presentations.

On these reality makeover shows, the subject is typically a willing participant, and understands that they have a problem. They just don't usually realize how unsustainable their status quo really is (yet).

The shows are structured not only to compel the show participant to "all-in" action, but also to tell a great story. The focus is 100% on the participant. These are all things great presentations do.

---

8   A.K. Pradeep, *The Buying Brain* (John Wiley & Sons, Inc., 2010) page 8, 18, 29

The interesting thing about all of these "makeover" reality shows is that they all follow the exact same choreography. **Your intention is essentially to give your audience a "makeover" through your presentation.**

One such example is a show on Netflix called *Queer Eye*. Originally debuting on Bravo back in 2003, the show features five experts (called the "Fab Five") on things like an individual's wardrobe, decorating, grooming, lifestyle, and food. With the current reboot of the series on Netflix, the show's premise has not changed; to rapidly address the issues the individual participant has and transform all aspects of their lives, helping them live it to the fullest.

Aside from the structure of the show, I will warn you...if you watch it, be prepared to cry. A lot. In the name of "book research," I certainly did.

Episode 1 features a fifty-eight-year-old man named Tom Jackson. Tom lives in a run-down apartment in the basement of a home, featuring an old, stained recliner chair. He refers to his favorite time of the day being when he can sit outside on his porch, have a cigarette, a "redneck margarita" (which was simply a Mountain Dew mixed with Tequila) and watch TV. He has been divorced three times, and is clearly a disheveled, unhappy mess.

The Fab Five arrive to a welcoming Tom, understanding his need to change. However, the team quickly shows him how his current situation is actually worse than he thinks, pointing to examples of how having just one place to sit in his home represents a challenge for any guests he may bring over, how his choice of clothing is impacting his confidence, all the way to how his hair conditioner is drying his scalp. Tom, while uncomfortable at times, quickly realizes that his situation is in need of help. Through the examples and the feelings the Fab Five bring to light, Tom is quickly "all in" and ready to begin his makeover.

Seventy-two-hours later, Tom is now a confident, well dressed, well groomed man with a stunning apartment, and a date with the love of his life: his third wife from whom he has since divorced, but with which he still shares a special relationship.

Thinking of the explanation and example above, but with your client's situation in mind, is there an opportunity to make your presentation all about your prospective client? To help the prospect understand that their situation may be broader than just the problems they outline for you? That's the goal, right? To help them understand their problem more fully, to inspire feelings that their status quo is less sustainable than they originally thought, to motivate them to change, and to connect them in a way where they want to change with you!

THE CHOREOGRAPHY

How many of you have a simple framework for how you craft your presentations? I am about to walk you through a step-by-step approach I use as a guide to creating a presentation with a focus on your audience. It is designed to disarm, educate, engage emotion to bring the audience together, and compel action. This choreography can also be used for any presentation where the objective is influencing and affecting change: sales, client success, funding, presenting to a board, presenting to employees, on-boarding, etc.

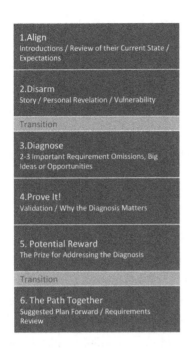

Fig. 8.1. A presentation choreography

STEP 1: ALIGNMENT

Begin the meeting with a verbal agreement on the purpose, agenda, and ground rules of the meeting. Remind everyone why they are in the room, and ensure there is consensus around the purpose.

The questions to ask yourself in preparation for this section are:

- Who is going to be in the audience, from both our side and their side?
- Why are our attendees specifically attending?
- If I were to ask the audience why they've invited us in to present to them, what would they say?
- What is their current buying state? Are they Actively Buying (AB), Passively Buying (PB), or Status Quo (SQ)?

In our reconfigured presentation with Whirlsung, we started the presentation with the normal introductions, discussing our understanding of why they brought us in. We were an upstart competitor to the company they were currently using for ratings and reviews. They were interested in exploring our company as a potential option for Whirlsung in the future (in a PB state).

We then asked each audience member to introduce themselves, along with why they were investing their time in the presentation. There is no better way to get alignment, and engage the audience's brain than by getting them talking from the beginning.

In this instance, we heard one audience member explain how she was simply there to learn, while another audience member explained that his perspective on Whirlsung's relationship with their current provider could be better, and he was looking for ideas. Other answers were similarly vague and protected, which is to be expected. The audience is wired to be in a protective mode, anticipating a presentation where they are about to be influenced, and not providing any clues as to the way they are feeling.

Nothing earth-shattering or new about this step in the presentation...it is likely how you currently execute your presentations.

STEP 2: DISARMING

The audience is getting ready to hear a sales pitch. Their brains are shifting into a mode that is subconsciously telling them, "Ok, we've gotten through the pleasantries, here comes the flood!" As we've reviewed, our brains are wired to resist being sold to or influenced, so when the brain is readying for a sales pitch, it subconsciously filters the incoming information with that in mind. Our purpose here is to disarm that filter, through a relevant story, a personal revelation, or a vulnerability.

The questions to ask yourself in preparation for this section are:

- Did anything fun happen while researching or preparing for this presentation we could share?
- Do we have any personal stories about our history with this company or their products?
- Is there something important this audience should know about you or your company that may become a concern for them?

The client is arming up their brains for the sales pitch. You're about to provide them with a diagnosis they likely weren't expecting, and if their guard is up, that message will take quite a bit more emphasis to hit the target. The disarming is about being human.

In preparation for the presentation, I'm making the assumption that you did your homework. You have researched their company, spent time on their website, and potentially interacted with the client as if you were a client yourself.

They are expecting you to say, "We did a lot of research in preparation for this presentation." What's unexpected is for you to tell a story about the research you did, and something funny that happened. Or, to tell them a story about your use of a product of theirs. Or, to talk about an element of a blog post they issued that really made an impact on the way you thought about them, their products, or your own world.

A few years ago, we were preparing a presentation for a Minnesota-based company called Fingerhut. (Fingerhut is an e-commerce shopping portal selling a wide range of products like furniture, electronics, and bedding that offers the option of receiving now while making monthly financed payments later.)

In this "Disarming" step, the sales representative from my team who was leading the presentation told a quick story.

"In preparation for today, we experienced what it is like to be a Fingerhut consumer. We purchased a product on your website, then experienced all of the interactions through delivery and the post-purchase interaction."

This rep, who sports the bald look day-to-day, passed around a picture of his children laughing hysterically at him wearing a *Rocky Horror Picture Show*-Frank-Furter wig. Essentially, it's a dark, curly, greasy looking wig that in today's age, wouldn't look good on anyone.

It was an incredibly funny, disarming, self-deprecating, and humanizing way to start the presentation. You could instantly feel the mood in the room change. The buyers who started with their guards up were now laughing. He didn't have to say another word about the amount of research and preparation that went in to the presentation. It was clear. And the audience was now ready to engage.

In the Whirlsung presentation, we chose to start with some vulnerability about our own company. We explained how, as an upstart competitor, there were pieces of our technology that were behind. We shared our understanding that they were our competitor's customer of the year, and had what our competitor considered a world-class implementation. The cards were stacked against us, and sharing that we were aware of this was disarming for everyone in the room.

TRANSITION

At this point in the presentation, the client is comfortable and disarmed. However, one wrong move, and your efforts to disarm their midbrain's "influence" protector will be lost. The audience may be readying for the self-serving portion of the presentation to begin, where you unload about how great you are. Instead, this transition is the opportunity to unexpectedly shift the conversation to how great THEY can be.

An effective way to make this transition is by communicating to the audience the "ah-ha" items that came up as you and your team prepared. "Before we dive in, in our research, we discovered two or three ideas which we believe could make a big impact. While we will address the requirements, would you like to spend a few minutes on those ideas?"

With Whirlsung, we transitioned with, "As we were preparing for this discussion, we discovered three potential opportunities where we felt there could be a major impact on your business. Can we briefly start there?"

With that type of introduction, the audience couldn't wait to hear what we had found. One attendee joked, "Great! Free consulting!"

STEP 3: DIAGNOSIS

Now is the time to teach them something about their business that they likely had not ever considered, showing them how their status quo is not only unsustainable, but worse than they may have previously considered. It's where you present them with the realization that a road must be travelled from where they are today, to where they need to be.

When you present, you should have done your homework. You understand your own products and services. You understand how those products are applied to companies like the one you are presenting to, and have a recommendation ready. This is where you show your confidence, your expertise, and something you learned from working with so many clients like theirs. Yes, you are actually smarter than the audience as it relates to your topic.

Whirlsung manufacturers appliances: refrigerators, washers and dryers, dishwashers, and countertop kitchen appliances. They sell their appliances through retailers like Home Depot, Lowes, Best Buy, Walmart, and many others. We understood that Whirlsung had issues with their current provider, and their requirements included seeking solutions to the holes that existed with their approach through those major retailers.

However, in our research, which included reading their annual report, we found that selling through the major retailers accounted for 55% of their revenues, while selling through "mom-and-pop" smaller retailers accounted for 45% of their revenues. We noticed that Whirlsung was not using our competitor's technology to address the remaining 45% of their revenue channel. As a matter of fact, they weren't using any technology at all in our category for that important element of their business. While we could have focused our presentation on helping the concerns they had prior to our presentation regarding the technology's application to the "55%" of their revenues, we covered their entire revenue generating business, representing a lift they hadn't even considered.

"We noticed that your approach with ratings and reviews is solely focused on big box retailers. You clearly recognize the value of having this type of technology in those environments, and the return you've received on that investment is obvious. However, while digging in, we noticed that just under half of your revenue is coming from smaller retailers, where that technology hasn't been applied. There's a major opportunity there."

This was opportunity number one. We had two more to share, but the attendees were deeply engaged with this one. It was time to back up our recommendation. Before we move to the "Prove It!" step, here are the questions to ask yourself in preparation for this section:

- During our preparation and research, are there any best practices that have not been included in the requirements we should suggest (and that we can address)?
    - A missed revenue opportunity?
    - A missed cost savings opportunity?
    - A potential risk to their business that they are potentially not seeing?
- If there was an RFP (Request for Proposal) as a part of the evaluation, simply put, what was missing from their requirements that they should be considering?

- In observing our own client base, are there two or three different or creative ways our clients are maximizing their results that would apply to this client? Do we have any big ideas to share?

STEP 4: PROVE IT!

Knowing that the brain needs data to justify a feeling they have in their own brain, we had to quickly follow up this feeling we created for Whirlsung with the proof. It was clear from our "Diagnosis" that Whirlsung hadn't considered the lower end of the market as having an opportunity. We provided them with some simple math to back up our recommendation.

"Using this technology for your major retailers has resulted in a considerable revenue lift. If we conservatively estimated that the revenue lift is 5%, and apply that to the smaller retailers, what would that mean to your business?" The answer was significant.

And, they felt their lift was actually higher than our conservative 5% suggestion. There was a lot of money on the table for Whirlsung to go after, and which they had not considered as an option before.

The questions to ask yourself in preparation for this section:

- Why, with data and logic, do we believe the idea presented in our "Diagnosis" is important?
  - What do we believe the revenue impact could be?
  - What do we believe the cost reduction opportunity could be?
  - What do we believe the reduction of risk impact could be?
- Why does the idea we presented in our "Diagnosis" apply specifically to this audience?

STEP 5: POTENTIAL REWARD

Considering that the human brain is more attracted to a reward than a potential future risk, the framing of this language is an important consideration.

With Whirlsung, we could have asked, "What happens if one of your competitors truly optimizes this channel of smaller retailers first? How would that impact your business?" This approach would reinforce the risk of not moving quickly. While this approach may work, framing that fear as a reward has a greater impact on attraction to an idea.

"What if you were to move first? How would those smaller retailers feel about one of their primary suppliers investing in them? How would that make the smaller retailers feel about you in comparison to your competition? How would it look to have Whirlsung appliances with hundreds of reviews on their websites, while your competitors have almost none? Your smaller retailers will love you."

The questions to ask yourself in preparation for this section:

- What can happen if this opportunity is prioritized, beyond the data and logic?
- What can happen if this opportunity is NOT prioritized?
- Remember that our brains are wired to make decisions with emotion and feelings. What are the feelings this opportunity can impact in terms of status, certainty, autonomy, relatedness, and fairness?

At this point in your presentation, you are likely in a truly collaborative conversation with your audience. Now is the time to go back to Step 3, and review your next idea. You haven't talked about your capabilities at all. And, when all is said and done, you've presented to the audience two to three ideas that they may have not considered. It is likely one of those ideas has struck a chord, however, all three have likely resulted in a fruitful discussion.

TRANSITION

During the Whirlsung meeting, one executive, who had told us at the beginning of the presentation that he would only be available for the first forty-five minutes of the ninety minutes we had scheduled, now committed to staying until the end.

In your presentation choreography, your audience has now likely recognized the opportunity in front of them, feels the potential reward for addressing this opportunity, and has done enough logical reasoning to justify the way they are feeling. You can now reveal the path to get them to this promised land.

STEP 6: THE PATH TOGETHER

The question to ask yourself in preparation for this section:

- How would we suggest addressing the "Diagnosis" ideas that resonated?

When presenting to the Whirlsung team, we put together a "here's how to proceed" framework. Simply put, we would put them on a platform that would address 100% of the retailers they sold through. We would provide a self-service technology that would address the 45% of smaller retailers, starting with one hundred licenses for free.

Before concluding the meeting, this "Path Together" included a reminder of our vulnerabilities. We were not perfect. We, like Whirlsung, had our own challenges to deal with. We said things like, "Whirlsung, you have a world class implementation with our competitor, so we understand the path may have speed bumps."

Whirlsung rolled up their sleeves, and we spent the next fifteen minutes discussing how we would handle those speed bumps...together.

Four months after winning the customer-of-the-year award from their current provider, Whirlsung was up and running with us. Contract signed. Competitor's contract cancelled. Technology implemented.

We were smaller, in terms of employees, in terms of customers, and in terms of proof. But we earned a tremendous amount of credibility through this process. To earn our way into the formal evaluation (which resulted in our win), we didn't have to take them through *our* story, *our* customer list, *our* office locations, or the awards *we* won. Because, compared to our competitor, our story would be less impressive. Instead, we gave them confidence in our ability to execute through making the entire presentation about what was possible in their world. We taught them. We told a great story. We disarmed them through our vulnerabilities.

OTHER "BRAIN" ITEMS TO CONSIDER

THE TED TALK

If the meeting where you will be presenting is scheduled for an hour or longer, resist the urge to attempt to fill the time slot entirely with your content. If you've done the choreography correctly, your presentation should take no longer than twenty minutes. Some recent studies claim that human beings have an attention span less than that of a goldfish, but I'm not convinced.[9] If you find in your preparation that the presentation is longer than twenty minutes, (a) it will not be effective, and (b) the content will not be retained. Cut it.

People learn in small chunks. The "sustained" attention span of an adult is thought to be no longer than fifteen to twenty minutes, and that's for someone performing surgery, handling fragile objects, or anything else requiring consistent results on a task over time. Listening to your presentation isn't likely to be that mission critical for your audience. It is said that even a surgeon forces

---

9   McSpadden, Kevin. Science: You Now Have a Shorter Attention Span Than a Goldfish. *Time*, 14 May 2015, time.com/3858309/attention-spans-goldfish/

themselves to disengage their brains, then re-engage every ten minutes or so to maintain focus.

When a person loses focus on their own, they can choose to re-focus, but it's our job to create that re-focus. When putting together your presentation, think about that concept. If the presentation has to be longer than twenty minutes, then think about how you can give the audience a brain rest every five to ten minutes. The best ways to do that are to tell a relevant story, engage the audience with a question or an activity, or anything else that forces the disengagement then re-engagement.

Watch a TED Talk to get inspiration. Each presentation is typically no longer than fifteen minutes, and in practically every instance, after fifteen minutes you've been moved to a new way of thinking, your brain isn't exhausted, and if there are any slides at all, they're purely visual (no or limited text). That's all on purpose. Don't think you need to be a world-renowned speaker to pull that off. You can do it!

YOUR SLIDES AREN'T YOUR SPEAKER NOTES

Remember that most people can't read and listen at the same time. If they're reading your text-laden slides, they're not listening. If your slides are covered in text, it will take a while for your audience to start listening to you. When possible, use pictures to emphasize your points rather than words. When putting together a presentation, try to build it out without using ANY slides first. Then decide what a slide can do to emphasize the points you're making. If you have to use text, keep them short. Don't use sentences unless you're showing a quotation or a definition. Also, keep in mind that most people can only hold around five items in short-term memory. If you have more than five bullets on a slide, the majority of the audience won't be able to remember them without re-reading the slide...which means they're not going to be listening to you.

Remember, your slides aren't your speaker notes.

YOUR LAST SLIDE SHOULDN'T BE A QUESTION MARK

Sadly, I've seen so many presentations where, at the end of the presentation, a slide that simply has a giant question mark, or a slide that just says "Questions?" prompts the Q&A session. Having your last slide, which stays on the screen during the final portion of a presentation, containing only the word "Questions?" is a mistake.

What is the primary point you want every audience member to remember when they leave the conference room?

What action do you want everyone in that room to take when they leave the conference room?

You don't need a slide that says "Questions?" to get the audience to ask questions. Ensure that everyone is consistent in their walk away. Not a long list of "next steps." Your last slide should contain your brief takeaway points. What are the two things you want every attendee to walk back to their desk remembering? The brain has a finite capacity to recall items from any learning event. While your participants may remember the "feeling" they had while listening, it is likely each participant will recall different, inconsistent "logic."

With Whirlsung, it was a simple sentence: "Bring the value of reviews to 100% of your retailers. Easy."

THE NEGATIVITY BIAS EXTENDS TO YOUR PRESENTATIONS, TOO

As we discussed in the Prospecting chapter on sending an email, your audience will not have the same level of excitement about your topic as you do. So, if you're presenting at a level 5, they are listening at a level 2 or 3.

Have passion for your topic. The words you use should be chosen to generate engagement. If you're passionate about the topic, don't bottle that excitement up...let it flow. Your audience will mirror your emotion. If you're excited and passionate about a topic, they will be more likely to be excited and passionate about it as well.

So much of that passion needs to come through in your first two minutes, when the audience is deciding whether to invest the cognitive attention to listen and engage. When practicing, record your first few minutes, then ask yourself while playing it back, "Would I want to listen to me for the time allotted?"

KEEPERS

- **Emotion binds, logic polarizes**: We discussed how, when we attempt to persuade someone with logic, we often end up solidifying their opposing position. However, through stories and emotion, groups of people come together. In a consensus sale with multiple buyers involved in your presentation, to bring a group together, focus on stories and emotion versus simply focusing on logic to make your case.

- **Create a "presentation choreography:"** Having a foundational, repeatable sales process is something most organizations start with. However, many organizations do not have a consistent framework for their presentations. We discussed the six-step presentation choreography framework designed to teach, tell a story, and reinforce both emotions and rewards for action.

- **Have empathy for your audience's brain**: The human brain's attention span is dangerously short during a presentation. Bring the energy, be concise, and know how to engage it through your stories and your slides.

CHAPTER NINE

EMPOWERING REFERENCES

BELIEVE IT OR NOT, BEING A REFERENCE COMES WITH SOME APPRE-
hension. First, it takes time, and typically falls pretty low on people's priority lists because it does not have a personal benefit. A reference wants to be helpful, but there's a line, and they need to focus on their day-job. Second, there's pressure associated with being a reference. They know what you've been through to get the prospect to this point in the selling cycle, and they don't want to screw that up. There's a feeling that a reference has that they need to sugar-coat the flaws, and present only the 5.0 speak that is expected from them.

If you're the buyer and you're speaking with a reference, you are looking for the honest, less than perfect reviews. If you can't get that, then the call was essentially a waste of time. The goal of the call is similar to reading through ratings and reviews on a product website: We are wired to seek out the negative along with the positive in order to get a full picture of what to expect post-purchase and can't make the decision until we have that full picture.

First, just like your prospecting emails, asking a client to be a reference must be framed as valuable for the client. If you're requesting that a client be a reference for you, make the request with empathy. A typical reference request might read, "I have a potential client who would like to speak with someone who's worked with us in the past. Would you be willing to be a reference for us?" This email starts with "We," and ends with "us." You are simply creating more work for your client, without helping them see the value in this request.

Instead, a better way to frame your request could be, "Would you be interested in speaking with the senior vice president at Acme Corporation? She has an incredible background, is evaluating our products, and would like to speak to someone about their experience. You immediately came to mind, as I figured there would be mutual value in a conversation with her."

Second, empower your references to talk through the challenges they've had in working with you. If they are an advocate for you, then they are likely to have a great story around how you and your organization addressed the issue, or at least plan to. Have the conversation with your reference that assures them that sharing your imperfections, with the goal of creating the feeling for the buyer that you are, in fact, a 4.2-4.5 and not a perfect 5.0, will make the call infinitely more valuable.

Lastly, knowing that it doesn't take a perfect reference to make a perfect reference call, is there an opportunity to develop more of your clients into potential advocates? In so many organizations, we're only willing to approach potential references that have had flawless experiences. Why not call the ones who didn't? Your clients will appreciate your efforts to help them build their network and share their successes. Your clients want you to be successful, so you would be surprised how many of these clients would be willing to help your organization, especially if it is valuable to them personally. If you are proud of the way you, as an organization, rallied around the issue, a negative experience can easily become a positive influence on a potential buyer.

KEEPERS

- **There's value to being a reference**: When asking a client to be a reference, stop positioning the call as a favor to you. Position the reference call as being mutually valuable, because it is.

- **Encourage your references to be transparent**: Let your client know that positioning you and your company as imperfect is okay. An imperfect reference is the most valuable reference to a potential buyer.

- **You have more potential references than you think**: With knowledge that imperfect references are valuable, and connecting clients with prospects is mutually valuable, there is an opportunity to develop more of your clients into references.

SECTION 4:

WHY NOW?

CHAPTER TEN

TRANSPARENT NEGOTIATIONS

"Try it! You'll like it."
–Alka Seltzer commercial from 1972

EVERY YEAR, OVER 7,000 INDIVIDUALS CONVERGE ON LAS VEGAS for the annual World Series of Poker. At every table, men and women from around the world sit across from each other, competing for the multi-million-dollar prize playing Texas hold 'em...a version of poker.

Hiding your "tells" is essential to playing successfully. A "tell" or "poker face" is a change in a player's demeanor that can reveal subconscious clues about how good of a poker hand they're holding. Wearing sunglasses, maintaining posture for mental alertness, and relaxing facial muscles are among the most common approaches to keeping a good poker face.

In poker, there is one winner. Everyone else at the table loses.

Now imagine walking into a poker tournament and beginning the round by throwing your cards face-up on the table.

In negotiation, those whom you are negotiating with are wired to resist influence similar to a sales engagement, and are anticipating a battle. "Transparent Negotiation" is showing your hand to the buyer from the beginning, disarming their barrier to the discussion. It's providing your buyer with the transparency that continues to build a feeling of certainty, fairness, and provides them with the autonomy to configure their own deal with you.

In many negotiation classes, similar techniques are taught to that poker example. Hiding your "tells" is often presented as an important element of maximizing the odds of a favorable deal. Many of these classes are two to three days in length, where you're taught such intensive techniques, you can probably hold your own in a massive union labor contract.

As it turns out, your transactions at work shouldn't be that complicated. You can negotiate a win-win agreement with limited training, and full transparency.

It's all in the "levers."

A few years ago, I was running sales for a small technology company based in Pleasanton, California. I had "Enterprise" reps spread around the United States who focused on large, complex selling cycles, typically in the low seven-figures. Our biggest clients were in discrete manufacturing industries, like automotive, aerospace and defense, and oil services companies.

David, my rep in Houston, called as he approached the finish line of a three-year, $2.5 million opportunity with a large oil services company. The buyer's procurement office contacted David, requesting a meeting with an executive who could make aggressive decisions, so I gladly obliged.

Upon arriving at the organization's offices, it was disturbing to see that all of the cars in the parking lot had backed in. I learned quickly that this policy was enacted in order to expedite an evacuation if one was ever required.

Very comforting.

David and I checked in, were greeted by an executive assistant, and escorted up an elevator. Upon arriving at the reserved conference room, we were surprised to find not one procurement representative, but an entire team of five procurement professionals waiting in a conference room. I'm pretty sure they were all drooling, ready to dig into us, but my memory is a touch hazy.

After exchanging a few pleasantries, I was pretty confident as to where this discussion was going to go. It was clear that a Texas hold 'em approach wasn't going to work. To disarm this hungry crowd of procurement professionals, I would need to let the tension out of the room through providing full transparency. So, instead of hiding our hand, my plan was to throw the cards face-up on the table.

Pointing to the dry-erase board in the room, I asked the group, "To make this discussion easier, do you mind if I use the whiteboard?"

THE "LEVERS"

After they agreed, I wrote the following four items on the whiteboard, known as our "levers;"

1. Volume
2. Timing of Cash
3. Length of Commitment
4. Timing of the Deal

As I wrote, I explained, "I know why you've asked us to come in today. My assumption is that you'll be asking us to get more aggressive with our proposal. To aid in the conversation, I thought it would be helpful if I shared the four things that matter to our business."

They expressed their appreciation and confirmed my suspicion. "In order for us to move forward, we'll need 35% off your proposal price," explained George, their head of procurement.

Instead of being flabbergasted by the request, wondering where a random number like 35% came from, the levers would quickly become our guide to the discussion.

After George took a moment to explain his request, I replied, "Well, using the levers I wrote on the board, I believe I have a path to get you there."

The mood in the room went from tense, untrusting, and divided to positive, open, and collaborative.

"Let's go through these one-by-one, as these elements represent not only how our pricing is configured, but also the levers that drive our business."

VOLUME

"Number 1 is Volume. The more technology/licenses/volume you're willing to commit to, as you might imagine, the better for our business. We're willing to pay you for that in the form of a discount."

That phrase, "pay you in the form of a discount" is one I used often. It sets the tone. It legitimizes the pricing we provided as a part of the initial proposal. And, it reminds the client at every stage of the discussion that we're not here to provide charity, but to structure a mutually beneficial agreement.

"The proposal reflects the number of licenses and technology you and your team have decided to begin with. As you can see in the proposal, there is a 15% discount included based on your volume commitment."

George chimed in, stating with a chuckle, "I know, I know. The 35% requirement is in-addition-to the already included discounts."

I replied, jokingly, "I figured." Adding, "As a part of our discussions throughout your evaluation process, we've explored opportunities to expand beyond this initial commitment, with a goal to eventually provide licenses to a broader audience at your company. If we're able to add more functionality and licenses to this initial transaction, we can potentially reduce the overall contract by as much as 10%."

One of the procurement team members, Jane, replied, "That's an interesting angle. However, because we have been in discussions for a few months, and had fully scoped the initial project, adding additional licenses or functionality would have to wait." It was clear they appreciated this suggested path to reduce the overall investment, however, we would have to put an "X" through the Number 1 on the whiteboard, and proceed to the next lever.

TIMING OF CASH

The three-year proposal as delivered included terms where the client would be required to make annual, up-front payments.

"Ok, well let's move on to Number 2, which is the Timing of Cash. Surprisingly enough, we like cash," I joked. "The faster you're willing to pay, the better for us. If you're willing to accelerate how quickly you pay us, we're willing to pay you for that in the form of a discount."

Prior to the meeting, I read through their public facing financial statements, seeing that they had literally billions of dollars in cash on their balance sheet.

"If you're willing to pay for the entire three-year commitment up-front, we're willing to pay for that in the form of a discount. We are willing to pay 5% off the entire contract for each year of accelerated payment, so 10% for the additional two years."

Beth, one of their procurement team members in the room, exclaimed, "Now that's interesting. We may be able to do that!"

I put a star next to the Number 2 on the whiteboard, then proceeded to the next lever.

LENGTH OF COMMITMENT

"Number 3 is the Length of Commitment. Having predictable, committed revenue is highly valuable to our organization. It allows us to make investments that you will benefit from in terms of technological innovation, and allows us to hire people for specific requirements when necessary. You'll obviously have contractual protections against underperformance, however, the longer you're willing to commit to the technology, the better able we are to pay you in the form of a discount."

The current proposal was for three years. I added that, for each additional year they were able to commit, we were able to pay in the form of a 5% discount for each year. So, a five-year commitment would result in an additional 10% off.

They responded with appreciation for that lever, but explained that in the oil services industry, commitments of even three years were difficult, so five years would be near impossible. However, they left the option on the table.

I added a question mark to the Number 3 on the whiteboard, then moved on to the last lever.

TIMING OF THE DEAL

"Number 4 is the Timing of the Deal. Our ability to forecast our business is incredibly valuable. It allows us to prepare the necessary resources, and the predictability an accurate forecast provides bolsters investor confidence. If we can agree on a target date by which we'll get the contracts done, we'll reward you for keeping to that date in the form of a discount."

This meeting took place on a humid, buggy July afternoon in Houston. With almost ten weeks left to the quarter, I added, "If you're able to finalize this agreement before the end of September, we're willing to pay you for that alignment with an additional 5%."

The procurement team looked at each other, agreeing that ten weeks should provide plenty of time to finalize an agreement, and happily added a star next to the Number 4.

I wrapped up this portion of the discussion by revisiting the levers on the whiteboard.

X) VOLUME - 10%

★2) TIMING OF CASH - 10%

?3) LENGTH OF COMMITMENT - 10%

★4) TIMING OF THE DEAL - 5%

"So far, we've gone through these four elements of our pricing. With Volume, we presented a path to an additional 10% off, but determined this was unlikely. With the Timing of Cash, we determined that payment up front for all three years of the agreement was a good option, providing a path to 10% off. The third lever was the Length of Commitment, and we mutually determined that extending to a five-year commitment would be difficult, even with an additional 10% reduction. And finally, we mutually agreed to align around the completion of this contract by the end of September, and for that alignment, we would provide an additional 5%."

After a quick repeat discussion around the Length of Commitment, the question mark quickly became an "X," and in a short period of time, we mutually had an agreement. "With that, we've provided a path to the 35% reduction you requested and have aligned around 15%; 10% for the accelerated payment, and 5% for the forecastability."

The procurement team agreed. Together we agreed to action items and next steps, leaving the discussion with the mutual feeling of a true partnership.

As David and I left the building, we talked about how to make this process even easier. I've never run a marathon before, but I can imagine that attempting to complete a marathon without having trained would be a painful experience. Instead, communicating your levers from the first discussions around your pricing model through to the proposal makes the negotiation "event" infinitely easier:

1. **During the "Positioning" phase**: At the start of the sales cycle, when a prospect asks about how our solutions are priced, be transparent right from the beginning. After briefly explaining the pricing model, explain that your pricing is also reflected in the levers: in this case, those levers are volume, timing of cash, length of commitment, and timing of the deal. Your levers are likely to be very similar, with the exception of "length of commitment," which may not apply if you sell a one-time item.

2. **Proposal Delivery**: When we deliver our initial proposal, it should be clear that your pricing is modeled around your levers. The dollar amount reflects the requested volume, annual up-front payments, a multi-year commitment, and is based on an agreement by a reasonable date.

3. **Final Negotiation**: Then, when it comes to the negotiation, the discussion is much easier. Often, it's unnecessary. The client already knows how to maneuver the proposal to reduce the price.

Driving your pricing and negotiation discussions leveraging transparency is an unexpected way to strengthen partnerships, and continue to build trust right through to contract signature. However, sometimes a curveball or two pops up during the process. The following are a couple of examples, and how to address them using the "levers."

"WILL YOU HOLD THE PRICE FOR ANOTHER WEEK?"

Sure enough, as we approached the end of September, the phone rang. It was David, explaining to me that George had just called him with the following ask: "We just found out that the signer will be on a cruise the final week of September, and unavailable to sign. Will you hold the price into the first week of October? I'm sure it will be signed as soon as he gets back."

When making a decision, certainty is a core feeling the brain desires. As a part of the negotiation we provided a discount associated with the certainty of the completion of the agreement by a mutually agreed upon date (in this case, the end of September).

When the buyer makes a request to extend that discount beyond the mutually agreed upon date, create uncertainty in your answer. David called George and simply said, "We do not know if we'll be able hold the price into October. What I *do* know is that this price is still valid through the end of September, so can we talk about October in October?"

By taking this approach, the previously agreed upon date is maintained as the "certain" option. Otherwise, the second you provide certainty regarding whether you will hold the price beyond the originally agreed upon date, you've charted your course:

- If you say yes to holding the price into October, then your deal just moved to October, and your levers of negotiation just lost credibility.
- If you say no, then your client will sense an erosion of the trust in the

partnership you've built throughout the process. And the client may tell you that if the price will change with a shift of the dates, they may have to take the agreement through the entire approval process again.

So, my advice to David was to create uncertainty in his answer, essentially reinforcing the *certainty* of what the price will continue to be based on the previously agreed to date. He delivered the message to George.

George responded by saying, "Well, ok. I'll do everything I can to still get this done, but there's a chance it won't happen, so we need to be prepared for that." David understood.

A few days later, David was holding a signed contract, three days before the end of September.

"WE CAN'T SIGN THIS AGREEMENT WITHOUT A TERMINATION FOR CONVENIENCE CLAUSE."

For most contracts where length of commitment matters, there are warranty provisions, or something called "termination for cause." Essentially, warranty and cause provisions provide buyers with protections in case the solution does not function as described in the documentation. However, many larger organizations ask for something called "termination for convenience." Termination for convenience (TFC) provides the right for the client to cancel the contract at any time, and for *any* reason.

When George asked for this, we were deep in the back-and-forth of the redline process on the contract. During the process, their legal team had added a paragraph referring to a TFC. We red-lined it out. They added it back in. So, we scheduled a discussion.

When addressing this request, I explained, "As we discussed when I was down in Houston, the 'length of commitment' element is vitally important to our business. The predictability a commitment provides is a key tenet of our business model, which is reflected in the agreed to pricing. Can you help me understand the requirement for termination for convenience, and under what circumstances you'd envision exercising it?"

George answered by explaining how they require protections in case the functionality isn't delivering as promised, the results aren't as promised, or the relationship isn't working out.

"George, remember that the contract has protections in case our solutions don't deliver as promised. Those are contained in the language under Warranty/ Termination for Cause," I replied. "If you need additional flexibility beyond those clauses, termination for convenience represents no commitment, so the pricing would need to be modified to reflect that, which would be in the form of our 'month-to-month' pricing. We can provide that pricing to you, but you're unlikely to like it."

George asked about the premium pricing they would need to absorb in order to include the TFC language in the contract. We explained that our month-to-month commitment pricing represented a 30% increase in their investment. George was surprised, however, the certainty and fairness associated with our use of the levers resulted in their decision that the flexibility TFC language provides wasn't worth the price. TFC was red lined out permanently.

KEEPERS

- **Identify your levers**: What is your pricing model based on? Ours was based on (a) how much the client buys (Volume), (b) how quickly the client was willing to pay (Timing of Cash), (c) how long the client was willing to commit (Length of Commitment), and (d) when the client executed the agreement (Timing of the Deal). Yours may be different. For many companies, these levers are exactly the same. However, in service categories, a volume lever may be replaced by service level commitments.

- **Assign value to your levers**: How much are you "willing to pay in the form of a discount" for each lever? You likely already have volume discounts built into your pricing model. However, how valuable is it to have cash up front, or multi-year agreements, or predictability in your forecast?
- **Enable your team**: Each team member should be able to rattle off your levers in their sleep.
- **Show your hand early and often**: Providing clarity and consistency from the first discussion on pricing all the way to the last negotiation will absolutely result in longer commitments, faster cash, more predictability, and quota attainment you can be proud of.
- **Allow your buyers to essentially roll their own deal**: This will continue momentum, trust, and get you value for every dollar you provide in the form of a discount.

CHAPTER ELEVEN

NEGOTIATING TERMS & CONDITIONS

"You must keep your mind on the objective, not on the obstacle."
– William Randolph Hearst

YOU'VE GONE THROUGH AN ENTIRE SALES CYCLE. IN MANY CASES and industries, it takes months or even years to get through the sales process with your potential buyer. Now, it's time for the lawyers to pound through the terms & conditions (Ts & Cs) so we can all sign the agreement and move on to the actualization phase.

The entire process leading up to the contracting point involves the build up of trust and confidence. They have the support of their team, it's the correct solution for their needs at the right time, and the value matches or exceeds the investment required. It's a feeling. They TRUST you and trust themselves.

In so many businesses, the momentum of the deal slows to a grinding halt at the finish line due to "Argh! The lawyers are involved!" All organizations involved have a vital responsibility to balance risk with the anticipated reward. Every organization invests a considerable amount into the legal portion of their budget to ensure that their liability in any contract does not create undue risk that could jeopardize the business itself. As a result, the legal process often makes it difficult to forecast the closure of your deal, and can impact sleep more than many other facets of the selling process. In some cases, the legal negotiations actually end the contract before it begins.

As a result of the grueling legal processes, the buyer's excitement level has often eroded by the time you get to the signatures. Momentum is lost. Trust is eroded. The final stage of the sales cycle/buying journey is sometimes the longest and most painful, especially when selling to large, multinational corporations.

Why does the legal process take so long for buyers and sellers? What can you do to help maintain momentum through the final stage of the cycle prior to signature?

Remember two things from previous chapters:

1. In every interaction with the client, you are either building trust or eroding trust. When trust drops, deals slow down, and risk to your sales opportunity enters the equation.

2. Clients want their relationship with you to be as easy as possible. The more effort, burden, or homework you give the client, the less confidence they have in the relationship.

Your lawyers are a part of your sales team, and the lawyers on the buying side are human beings evaluating how much they can trust you while averting mentally strenuous activities. Sales teams regularly treat the legal process like it's not a part of the sales process and relinquish control of that portion of the cycle.

It's time to blend your legal process into your sales process and use your Ts & Cs contract as a sales tool to maintain momentum, trust, and control in the cycle.

START IN THE MIDDLE

The contract process typically starts with a document provided by you, the seller. This document contains the terms and conditions that outline what can and cannot be done in the relationship, term length and termination options, liability and indemnification conditions (aka, whose fault is it when something breaks), and a number of other items meant to clarify what happens if something goes wrong. The entire point of the document is to protect the parties when the other party screws up. Not a fun way to finish a transparent sales cycle, no?

The document is typically delivered via email, with an email communication from the seller to the buyer stating, "Here is our master agreement. Let me know when you expect to have the first set of redlines completed." In some cases, the seller will communicate to the client that, in typical cases, they do one round of redlines, then schedule a phone call to go through the remaining open items in hopes of finding a satisfactory middle ground. In other words, "I'm sending this long, brain-exhausting document over the fence to you. You're not gonna like it, so let us know when to expect hell on Earth to begin."

But you actually have an opportunity to build trust the first time you send the legal document to the buyer.

Let's start with the language. Does your legal language favor you over the buyer? Go through it paragraph by paragraph. Are there conditions that are less than fair, but that you hope the buyer just accepts? Are there items that get red-lined and negotiated every single time?

Take, for example, language around a contract "auto-renewal." If you're selling in a world where a buyer signs up for a term (i.e., a subscription over a definitive time period), and at the end of each term, the buyer and seller need to reconvene to renew the agreement, then you may desire to put "auto-renewal" language in the contract. Essentially, the language states that the contract will automatically renew for a defined period unless cancellation takes place prior.

Language like this is helpful for both parties. It saves time and it provides foresight into budget requirements for future terms. However, I often see two things vendors do that erode trust through this term:

1. They sneak in a requirement that says the buyer needs to provide over sixty days of notice prior to the end of their term if they intend to cancel.

2. There's no discussion with the buyer regarding the mutual value of the language (or any other language, mind you) before sending over the document.

There's an opportunity to differentiate yourself with the buyer's legal team here. Your buyers deal with many, many vendor contracts. And the majority of vendors handle the process exactly the same...throwing the contract over the wall.

When it comes to auto-renewal language, here's what the vendor typically proposes:

"The term of this Agreement is three (3) years commencing on the Effective Date, unless terminated sooner in accordance with this Agreement (the "Term"). **Thereafter, the Term will be extended and renew on a year-to-year basis, unless either party gives written notice to the other not later than ninety (90) days before the end of the then Term of its intention to terminate.**"

Here's what they're telling the client (think about whether you think this would increase trust): "**Thereafter, the Term will be extended and renew on a year-to-year basis, unless whoever is in your position three (3) years from now forgets or isn't aware that this language is buried in this 15-page document. I won't be here, anyway, so good luck, jackasses!**"

This language places an unfair burden on the client and benefits the seller more than the buyer. Auto-renewal language is, in fact, valuable to both parties. If you want to continue to build momentum and trust through the finish line of the deal, add a line to the end of this paragraph that says, **"The ninety (90) day notification requirement for the contracting party will only be valid if the selling party reminds the contracting party of this provision 120-180 days prior to the end of the term."**

Where are you eroding trust in your contractual language? Where you are placing a burden on your client? This historical approach to legal discussions explains why so many larger companies are forcing vendors to start from their document, placing the burden entirely on the vendor. They want easy—just like you, and every other human brain. By starting with their own documents, they force the vendor to start on their end of the field, knowing that working towards the middle will never happen.

A few other tips for getting through the legal negotiations:

- **Start in the middle**: Create a legal document chock-full of unexpected surprises that create mutual value and scream partnership.
- **Have a cover document**: Create a cover document of a few bullets that lay out how the contract was created, what the overall terms are, and explains the reasoning behind language that may appear on the surface to be one-way, but serves to benefit both parties mutually.

Legal teams are always stretched thin. Their job requires a tenacious focus and attention to detail. They are required to analyze every sentence, imagine what *could* happen, then decide whether a change is required...an exhausting task to do repeatedly, day after day. This approach will certainly speed your sales cycles, differentiate your organization, and continue to build trust right through to contract signature.

KEEPERS

Transparency and control doesn't need to stop when the lawyers start the paper-work process.

- **Identify your self-serving terms and conditions**: Can they be explained via a cover sheet that is delivered with your contracts? Should those terms and conditions to be modified to be less self-serving?
- **Provide opportunities for unexpected honesty in your terms**: If your language puts a burden on the buying organization, seek ways to reduce the burden. Find ways in your language to help the buying organization feel as though they will maximize the value of a relationship with you, and you will help them.

SECTION 5:

WHY STAY, BUY MORE & ADVOCATE?

CHAPTER TWELVE

POST-PURCHASE INTERACTION

"There can be as much value in the blink of an eye
as in months of rational analysis."
–Malcolm Gladwell, *Blink*

YOUR BUYER FINALLY SIGNED THE CONTRACT. YOU CELEBRATED the victory in your office with your fellow sales team by whichever ritual you have established, like banging the "new sale" gong, ringing the bell, blowing off the blow horn, shaking the tambourine, dinging the triangle, strumming the harp, or cracking open the champagne.

All of the stars aligned for the buyer. The solution addresses their problem. The timing was right. The investment matched their perceived value. The signor had the authority to sign. And, most importantly, the buyer felt like all of the important boxes in their brain had been checked. Transparency was essential to all of those steps.

But what happens next is just as important as what you've already been through. The first days post-signature will likely determine whether they buy more from you, stay with you long term, refer you to others without being asked, and call you first when they join their next company. Don't let them fall off the trust mountain.

Often, when we are compensated for closing a deal, we "throw" the client over the wall to the delivery team responsible for implementing whatever the buyer just purchased. In many organizations, the salesperson's last interaction of substance with the client takes place on the day the contract was signed. Then, a whole new team is assigned, and the trust-building process starts over.

World-class sales organizations and sellers don't stop when the deal is signed. The momentum and trust continue to build while the ink is still drying. Your buyers just allocated a chunk of their budget vital to you and your organization. They are more on the hook now than they were before they signed. It is your job to maintain that momentum and continue to grow the trust.

Is there any better lead than a referral from a happy customer? In my experience, more than 75% of our new customers have historically come from our existing customers. Do you want those kinds of leads to arrive in your inbox every day? Don't give up control after what you perceive to be the finish line: the signed contract. For an organization to experience rapid growth, they must ensure that trust is transitioned, versus thrown over the fence to be rebuilt by another part of the organization. Here are some tips on how to do this.

THE POST-SALE LETTER

As a buyer, when you've made a purchase of substance, the endorphins associated with that purchase are still there, wearing off slowly. You're telling your friends about the purchase you just made, and how excited you are to realize the benefits of that investment. The worst thing that can happen is not hearing a peep from the seller for days, weeks, or in some cases, a month or more. This is why you often get an email confirmation in your inbox within seconds of confirming your transaction.

As a seller, work with your internal teams to establish a communication process that starts from the minute the signature is made. In its simplest form, that may be a letter that goes out immediately confirming their purchase, outlining what they've bought, and documenting the process that will take place. That process should include details on when they should expect to be contacted, and a kickoff call should ideally be scheduled within 24-48 hours of signature.

THE KICKOFF

If purchases require a kickoff call, it's your job to arm that team to maintain the momentum from the sales process. Spend fifteen minutes to give your team some background about the client, and what they are hoping to accomplish through the purchase, both professionally, but also personally. Your implementation team should be armed and ready to help your buyer accomplish their goals, not just make sure the solution is implemented properly.

For the kickoff call itself, your participation is vital. Many of the participants will not have met you yet, as they were not involved in the sales and evaluation process. Prepare a talk track to kick off the call that touches on the following points:

1. **The buyer's objectives**: Why did they invest the time and energy in evaluating solutions? What problem are they trying to solve? What is the potential impact of not doing anything? What is the potential impact of getting this right? Speak on behalf of the client.

2. **Why the buyer chose you**: Why did the buyer choose you versus the alternatives? Take a moment to briefly explain.

3. **A reminder of exactly what they purchased, and what they did not**: Aligning everyone during this first discussion will get everyone on the same page about what was agreed to, contracted for, and what support they are going to receive.

4. **Introductions to your team members**: As a seller, you want to give off the impression that you and your organization have configured a team that meets their needs. Introduce each of your implementation team members with their expertise, and then allow them to start building trust by having them relay an understanding of the goals of the project.

From there, it's time to step back and allow the process to unfold. Your implementation team will need to earn trust and take ownership of the relationship themselves. However, that doesn't mean that the sellers disappear. The best sellers schedule quick check-in calls with the buyer to assess their perception of the process. This communication may take place via email, too, where you're showing an active interest in their success. It really doesn't take much time, and the payoff from a successful onboarding experience will absolutely result in more opportunities, whether they be directly from the buyer or through referrals. Remember, those buyers change jobs, too, and you'll want them advocating for you and your organization when they turn their job over to someone else and move on to their next role.

KEEPERS

- **Your level of trust cannot end with the signing of the transaction**: Your current job is unlikely to be your last job. In many cases throughout my career, people have called me from their new jobs because they remember or know me from their last one.
- **Do not lose focus on a client after the contract has been signed**: Ensure that if a handoff is required, you handle it as a transition, not a throw-over-the-fence to whichever team in your company is "responsible" for the client's success.
- **Take the time to invest**: These handoffs and transitions will pay off through incoming leads throughout the rest of your career.

CHAPTER THIRTEEN

CLIENT SUCCESS

"Trust takes years to build, seconds to break, and forever to repair."

–Anonymous

I N MY ROLE AS THE CHIEF REVENUE OFFICER AT A SOFTWARE AS A service (SaaS)-based technology company, my responsibility was much broader than sales. The role of the chief revenue officer is to have oversight across the entire customer journey. Essentially, the role is about maximizing the revenue capacity of the organization by optimizing the end-to-end process for the client.

Focusing on customer experience was vital to our growth, and as a result, we had a team dedicated full time to the success of our clients. As you might imagine, this team was called our "Client Success" team. This team woke up every morning excited to help clients maximize their investment, maximize their own goal attainment, and grow their own careers in the process.

Essentially, whether your client success team has a quota or not, they are still occupying an important sales role. Client success teams are directly or indirectly responsible for:

- **Building trust with every interaction**: This team builds relationships. Different than a "technical support" team fielding individual issues, this team served to consult with clients, maximizing the return they receive from an investment in your products. As discussed throughout the book, as trust goes down, the amount of homework the client does goes up. A client who has purchased from you is subconsciously evaluating their level of trust in you throughout your relationship in much the same way. If the client doesn't trust your organization, they evaluate alternatives. When they evaluate alternatives, they often leave.

- **Uncover and position upsell and cross-sell opportunities**: Client success may not be driving individual sales cycles to the finish line, but they are the key to uncovering new, additional opportunities within the existing accounts they interact with.

- **Advocating for the customer within your internal organization**: Your client success organization is the voice of your clients within your organization. While your product team may want to speak directly to clients, the quickest path to alignment with your new product development team is through your client success team.

- **Escalations**: When a client is having a high priority problem, the client success organization becomes the key to how that experience is resolved, helping the organization understand the seriousness of the issue and set priorities.

YOUR CUSTOMERS DON'T WANT TO TALK TO YOU

According to the National Fire Protection Association, the nation's fire departments responded to 31.6 million calls in 2013.[1] How many of these calls were made because someone wanted to have a chat or talk about the weather? When you have to make a call to a fire department, it means you're likely having a bad day.

If you work in client success, you are the fire department of your company. A call from a client also often means something is not working right.

---

1   Keisling, Phil. "Why We Need to Take the 'Fire' Out of 'Fire Department'." Governing Magazine, July 2015, www.governing.com/columns/smart-mgmt/col-fire-departments-re-think-delivery-emergency-medical-services.html

In the brain, every interaction your client is having with you to resolve an issue they are having, no matter how fantastic a job you're doing to resolve the issue, is actually *reducing* their satisfaction. The brain craves autonomy. When something that did not require the assistance of others now does, it's unwelcome added work.

Here are two important pointers for client success teams:

1) INVEST IN SELF-SERVICE ISSUE RESOLUTION:

Ensure that your customers have the means to take care of issues on their own, easily. Simple, intuitive documentation on your website, or short YouTube type videos that walk clients through common troubleshooting are a key way to reinforce transparency and increase trust.

2) DON'T SEND CLIENT INTERACTION SURVEYS AFTER TROUBLESHOOTING:

After troubleshooting, many organizations will send out a survey asking "How did we do?" In doing this, you are actually reminding the client that they had an issue to be resolved, helping to commit the issue to their long-term memories. It's a subconscious double-whammy of negativity, even if your organization ultimately solved their problem.

Instead, send post interaction surveys after business reviews, trainings, or well-being checks. Use surveys to (a) reinforce the memory of the interaction type, then (b) use the learnings from those surveys to continually optimize how you execute those types of calls.

WHY ARE THEY REALLY ENDING THEIR RELATIONSHIP WITH YOU?

One of the bad things about working with renewable periods is that clients are constantly coming and going. If you have 1,000 customers and a 5% churn (meaning 5% leave every year), that means between three to five clients are leaving per month. That's around one per week. As clients notified us of their intent to leave, often I would jump on the phone with the key contact at the client to understand what happened, attempt to save the client from having to rip and replace by solving the issue, but ultimately take every churned client as an opportunity to learn and improve.

When discussing the "why" with these clients, I quickly noticed that the majority laid on the logic for their move.

"Well, Todd, we just weren't seeing the lift in conversions as a result of the use of your technology. From an ROI perspective, we simply couldn't justify the continued investment this year, and are going to try one of your competitors instead." Sounds very logical, right?

I put the phone on mute, looked over at the other team members in the room with me, and said, "That's not why they're leaving us."

I responded to the departing client, "That makes sense, and I appreciate your candor. Given that we know your priorities, and considering the technology is essentially the same from one vendor to the next, putting in a like-for-like solution would seem like a lower priority project. Can I ask what happened?"

He hesitated to answer...and I waited patiently. You could hear a bit of, "Uhhh, I really don't want to get anyone in trouble" from his eventual response.

He started in, "Todd, you and your team have been great. Please know that. However, some of our team members feel as though we're lost amongst all of your larger clients. Your team gives us instructions and advice but doesn't spend the time to help us really absorb the recommendations, and at times has seemed frustrated with us."

There it was. The reason wasn't about the ROI, it was about how our team made their team feel. He struggled to communicate the real issue. This feeling was something we could talk about, addressed in a way that mattered for them, and help our team improve. It was different than his first explanation, right? He had given us the truth about why they're making this investment in time and resources. We didn't make them feel the relatedness, status, and autonomy they desired. All feelings...and he actually used the word "feel" in his revised answer.

It's impossible to fix things you don't know about. When clients leave, getting to the heart of the "why" is a fundamental requirement. Listen for the "feel" when talking with a departing or upset client. If they're giving you logic, confirm that their logic is fully understandable, but don't be shy about getting to the real "why." Try this: "What you've said makes a lot of sense, and we regret not creating a better outcome for you. This is a big decision. Can you tell us what happened? What was the trigger that pushed you over the top?"

Don't be afraid to ask. When you hear answers that communicate a loss of their feelings of things like certainty, autonomy, and fairness, you're beginning to get to the heart of the issue.

CONFLICT AND THE BRAIN

It was 1998. I was the account manager for a massive manufacturing organization who had spent almost $20 million on our technology, plus as much as three times the technology cost just to implement the software in technical services. In my role, I was the day-to-day contact for account issues (not technology issues) and interacted with some group within the buyer's organization every single day.

The implementation was a massive undertaking. The technology was being installed on giant computer servers at their headquarters location, and required a great deal of coding, customizing, and configuring. It was a nine-month implementation, with a plan that was detailed down to the day.

As a part of the plan, there were two weeks set aside just before "go-live" called "testing." They planned to "go-live" over Labor Day weekend; being a major manufacturer, they wanted the extra day for the long weekend just to be sure.

Well, unfortunately, during the first few months of the process, the reality was that the implementation was behind by about ten days. However, the client demanded that the "go-live" still take place over the Labor Day weekend. So, a decision was made to sacrifice a large portion of the "testing" prior to launching the software to run the business. So, instead of two weeks to test, testing was reduced to just three days.

On the Friday before Labor Day weekend, the president of my organization walked down to my cube to check in with me.

He asked, "Everything on track and looking good for the go-live this weekend?"

I replied, "Yep. They're just finishing up testing and will be flipping the switch this weekend. By Tuesday morning after Labor Day, they will be running their operations on our software."

Tuesday morning, following the long weekend, the front page of the *Wall Street Journal* had an article about how this major manufacturer's organization had ground to a halt, and was completely shut down due to a massive software implementation failure.

Yep...front page of the *WSJ*. Now, over twenty years later, that former president still jokes with me about that situation when I see him. "Hey Todd, remember when you told me how everything was fine, and two days later [the client's products] were lined up and down the expressway?" Hilarious, Ed!

Don't get me wrong: this was no laughing matter when it happened.

When a client is boiling, the conversation can go one of two ways: towards a massive lawsuit, or towards a quick resolution and a round of beers where we all lick our wounds together. How you handle that first conversation makes ALL the difference.

Here's the brain trick: When a client is in full escalation mode with their emotions, the key focus is to change the "tense" of the conversation. They are likely to be in the "past tense" when they're exploding, with exclamations like, "How could you have let this happen?" and "You promised us that everything was all set for 'go-live' " and "This is all your fault!"

You must seek to change the tense from "past" tense to "present," then "future" tense as quickly as possible. How do you do this?

1) OWN THE PAST:
While you could go into a dissertation about how you warned the client about the costs of rushing into going live, if you do this, the client's brain will go into full survival/defense mode. Instead, *quickly* confirm that this is your responsibility. You are a 4.2-4.5, not a perfect 5.0. Own it.

Even if it's a ridiculous thing to own, and that the client admits to some responsibility, owning it disarms the defense mechanism immediately. The client may argue the opposite with you at this point, which is what you want. You may hear, "Todd, I appreciate you and your organization owning responsibility here, but we know we had some fault here."

Your response? "You made an investment leveraging us, and that investment is failing right now. Let's discuss what we can do about it right now."

That sentence quickly acknowledges the past, but moves to the present tense. And, if you're arguing because you want to own the blame, and the client now wants to own some of the blame, too, you did your job here!

Move quickly through this ownership, as the goal is to change the tense.

2) COMMUNICATE THE PRESENT:

Move quickly into outlining what you and your team are doing right now. Confirm what you need the client to focus on to fix the problem.

3) CONFIRM PLANS FOR THE FUTURE:

Promise a full debrief at a later time. If the client is asking for a promise of retribution in the form of credits or contract termination, now is not the time to discuss those items.

As it turns out, in the case of the manufacturing organization, one small syntax error in the middle of literally hundreds of thousands of lines of code caused the plant to shut down. One of our team members re-read every line of code, skipping sleep, and found it. It was a third party developer who made the error, so in the end, it was neither party's direct fault, but we owned it, and the organization is still our client, over twenty years later.

This was an extreme example, but client escalations happen every single day. When communicating voice-to-voice, practice this approach to changing the tense when a client is seeking someone to blame, and you'll find that your conversations are considerably more constructive and positive.

Although our organization could have cast the blame on the manufacturing company for shortening the test period, our approach to owning the issue, taking our best coders off of other projects to take a look, and having them work around the clock to find and fix the issue, resulted in a satisfied client.

QUARTERLY BUSINESS REVIEWS OR "QBRs"

If you conduct "Quarterly Business Reviews" (QBRs) periodically, or if scheduled check-ins are a core component of a client's journey, be sure to read through Chapter 6 again. Often, client success organizations that need to justify their results (or lack of results) will configure these business reviews with clients to be all about themselves.

"Look at all of the great things we did for you this year! Look at all the cases we closed. Look at all of the meetings and on-sites! Look at how great our technology worked!"

Instead, focus the choreography just like I outlined in Chapter 8, Presenting. Show what the client has done through your solution as a part of the alignment. You do not need to spend a great deal of time here, as the effectiveness of a QBR isn't determined by how good you make the client feel; it's about ensuring expectations are being met, and exploring opportunities to achieve even more.

Once you're through the alignment, if there is any elephant in the room, bring it up next. It's time to disarm. Is there a big issue outstanding? Did the delivery go awry? What problems arose over said period? Throw that grenade and disarm the clients. What happened, how was it addressed, what did we do wrong, what lessons were learned from it, what is the plan going forward...in that order.

Next is the time to press the client like a personal trainer would for one of their clients. Whether or not the client has achieved everything they could, it's now your job to show them how they can achieve even more. Like a salesperson would do, present the opportunity that they haven't prioritized using the presentation choreography.

"Here are three primary recommendations that we believe will help you achieve even more that you thought you could."

Lay out recommendation Number 1, then drive the point home with the logic (data, potential) and the potential reward. Do the same with recommendations Number 2 and Number 3.

From there, with agreement, you can outline the go-forward plan and get on with realizing the value that can be had.

Again, QBRs are NOT about you patting yourself on the back. Pat the client on the back for what they achieved.

KEEPERS

- **Remember how decisions are made**: Decisions are made with feelings and emotion and justified with logic. In client success, clients leave all the time that are getting a great ROI on their investment.
- **Listen thoughtfully**: When a client is threatening to leave, listen for the difference between the logic and the emotion. If there's no emotion, find it!
- **Be cognizant of emotion in all of your interactions with your clients**: When doing NPS (Net Promoter Score) surveys, ask a question about how they feel about the interactions with your company beyond just the results. Ask your sponsor, with your company name inserted in, "If I were on your team, talking about [company] at lunch, what would the conversation be like?"
- **The trust building never ends**: It is incredibly important when things inevitably go wrong.

BONUS CHAPTER

CHAPTER FOURTEEN

TRANSPARENCY APPLIED TO...

...YOUR JOB SEARCH

Consider transparency when you're interviewing for your next role. During an interview, you're *selling* yourself to the potential hiring manager...aka, the buyer. How do you apply these techniques to selling the greatest product of all: you?

Bad news. You have flaws. For many years, I was taught to hide my flaws in an interview, waiting until asked what my weaknesses are. Many are taught to answer this question with a strength disguised as a weakness.

"Well, I've been told I just work too darn hard. I get so passionate about my work, that I put my heart and soul into it. People have told me that I should get a hobby, but work has always been my hobby."

"I'm self-critical, in that I demand top performance in myself. Everything I deliver, whether it be internally or external, is a reflection of me, and therefore I make sure that it's a representation of my work ethic and drive."

"I had a weakness, but I fixed it. Now my weakness is that I don't have any weaknesses."

Ok, nobody has ever answered the question that way.

Put yourself in the hiring manager's shoes. You are attempting to influence this hiring manager (aka, "buyer") to buy from you, to buy that you're the ideal candidate for their role. This approach should be the same as a selling situation, where you're attempting to drive the trust level up near 100% and create less homework for the buyer to do on their own.

Instead of trying to create an "I'm a perfect 5.0, buy me" impression, there is every reason to create the impression that you are, in fact, a 4.2-4.5 in order to drive a better outcome.

Look at the job description. If you were interviewing you, what would you be concerned about? Your lack of experience in a given area? The gap in your resume? Your missing advanced degree?

Instead, be ready to be transparent from the beginning. Approach the interview in much the same way you would approach a discussion as outlined in Chapter 6, Positioning.

When the interviewer asks, "Why are you the perfect candidate for this role?," you would create an incredible amount of trust, connection, and acceleration in coming to a mutual decision about the role if you replied, "Well, let me start with why I may not be the perfect candidate for the role. In reading the job description, the majority of the requirements are a great fit for my experience, expertise, and passion. However, there are two here we should probably address right from the beginning." Let's say it's your lack of an advanced educational degree and a lack of required experience specific to the role. Why not say, "I see that a requirement is that I have a master's degree, and I'm sure you can see that I don't have one. I also fall just short of the required years of experience in a similar role. Let's address those first, then dive in to the other areas, ok?"

You'd be amazed at how disarming that is. Don't let the buyer figure it out on their own.

As hirers, we want to trust those who we employ. It's likely the most important feeling we will need to have to make a decision in your favor. As an interviewee, own the conversation, build trust from the beginning, and present yourself as a 4.2-4.5.

...YOUR RECRUITING

Whether or not you're a fan of the National Football League (NFL) or not, you've probably heard of the "NFL Draft." In what is the professional football league's most substantial source of adding players to their teams, each of the thirty-two NFL football teams are able to select the rights to an amateur player that is typically coming out of a university football program. At its most basic level, draft picks are made in an order that is set according to each team's performance in the previous season.

Teams start scouting next year's talent the day after the current year's draft. It's that important! These scouting department staff members have substantial budgets, and spend their time watching these potential recruits play in college, high school, and in some cases, since middle school. While in-game studies are very important, they're also analyzing their off-the-field behaviors, study habits in college, and their demonstrated levels of intelligence. Then there is the NFL Scouting Combine. At the Combine, over 300 potential draftees are brought in by invitation-only for a series of intense testing. They each must perform timed speed tests, weight-lifting analysis, jumping, shuttling, and sit through interviews, physical examinations, evaluations like the "Cybex test" (which tests joint mobility) and the "Wonderlic test" (an intelligence test).

The results? In an analysis of the past twenty years of player drafting, with all of those recruiting resources, all of the observations of these candidates, and all of the testing:

- 16.7% of the players drafted never ended up playing for the team that drafted them;
- 37.0% of the players drafted were considered a "bust," meaning they were never able to make a positive contribution to the team; and
- 15.3% of the players drafted were considered "poor," meaning that while they may have had flashes of solid performance, their tenure with the team was deemed "underwhelming."[1]

That's an even 69% of professionally-recruited players that essentially fail on their athletic endeavors.

Whether you're an external recruiter running your own firm, or you're a part of an internal recruiting firm, that's what you are up against. You don't have the benefit of intensive data analysis, observation of candidates in their previous jobs, days with them off-site before hiring, or a massive battery of tests. Yet, you're on the hook to fill roles that could make-or-break the organization you work for.

In scrolling through my LinkedIn timeline this morning, I came across this post from a recruiter:

"Looking for 'A' players. Former executive from Salesforce / SAP / Oracle needs reps who consistently perform at the top 10% of their teams with a Rolodex of Fortune 100 accounts. This one is on fire! 100% growth, VC backed in the 'AI' space. $175k base / $175k variable with 20,000 options. $1M+ W2. Who's ready???"

Now, I wasn't a math major in college, but $175,000 + $175,000 doesn't equal $1,000,000. And this wasn't the only post like it. My radar went up. Does yours?

1   Ludford, Warren. "Most NFL Draft Picks Are Busts." Daily Norseman, 13 Apr. 2017, www.dailynorseman.com/2017/4/12/15274148/most-nfl-draft-picks-are-busts

As a recruiter, if you're presenting a role or a candidate as a perfect 5.0, your buyers (the recruits or the hiring managers) will immediately be resistant. And, consider presenting your open roles as though they are a 4.2-4.5.

I know some fantastic recruiters, and I recently had coffee with one of them: Gregg Salkovitch, the principal of a recruiting firm in Chicago. Gregg told me a story of a role he was seeking to fill for a client he had years ago, who was interested in hiring one of his candidates (we'll call him "Josh"). Through the process, Gregg came to the realization that Josh had a negative vibe. Most of his conversations with Josh included a healthy dose of complaining, and it became clear that he had some things to work on.

During Gregg's next conversation with the client, who happened to be the chief operating officer of a substantial company, Gregg said bluntly, "I don't think you should hire Josh."

The COO, flabbergasted by Gregg's proclamation and knowing how the recruiting game has been traditionally played, replied, "What's your angle? You must have another client to send him to who's paying you more."

Gregg explained to me how insulted he was initially by the insinuation that he was playing some sort of game by talking his client OUT of hiring one of his candidates. Essentially, Gregg was taking money out of his own pocket, but this COO assumed the opposite—that Gregg had found a way to make even MORE money on this candidate.

"Shocked by transparency" is what Gregg called it. This wasn't an attack on him specifically, but it was the result of many recruiters, salespeople, or others in positions of influence who have chased the check, instead of the relationship.

Unexpected honesty became a foundation of his relationship with the client. Over time, Gregg continued to help, and as of this writing, is working through a contract extension to continue to provide services for them. When you find a recruiter who not only says they're looking out for your best interests, but proves it in every interaction, you hold on to them.

...YOUR REQUESTS FOR PROPOSALS

Ever bought anything while you were drunk? Every known anyone to make a significant purchase while intoxicated that they later regretted?

As it turns out, this is pretty common.

When you've had a drink or two (or three or four), alcohol lowers inhibitions in the logic center of your brain (the neocortex) and heightens emotions in the feeling center (the midbrain/limbic). That change in balance makes for potential disaster. As a matter of fact, a study showed that more than $30 billion was spent by inebriated Americans in 2017.[2] Interestingly, men spent more than twice the amount that women did while drunk in that period.

What does that mean to you, given you likely won't be driving decisions by pouring alcohol down the gullet of your buyer?

As recently as the 1990s, it was common to see purchase processes happening out on golf courses, at restaurants, attending shows, or at sporting events. Over the past twenty years, many companies have stopped accepting gifts from vendors. In many cases, buying organizations will no longer accept invitations to events, and often no longer allow a vendor to pay for their lunch. The organizations understand how decision making is made, based on feelings, which are often exacerbated by alcohol. The need for formal, logic-based decision making in purchasing organizations is now as intense as it has ever been, and as a result, the RFP (request for proposal) was born.

---

2   Bloom, Jonathan. "Study Shows Americans Spend Billions Shopping While Drunk." ABC7 San Francisco, 7 Mar. 2018, abc7news.com/shopping/study-shows-americans-spend-billions-shopping-while-drunk/3187953/

An RFP is a logic-based document used by buying organizations to solicit a formal proposal from vendors for a potential purchase. A typical RFP has a long list of requirements, where vendors are required to provide yes-or-no answers to each requirement listing the affirmation of their ability to satisfy the specific requirement. Its use is meant to reduce the ambiguity of a purchase through specific, logic-based, yes-or-no questions.

An RFP's use has proven to enhance the amount of logic used to justify a decision, but does not eliminate the fact that decisions still get made with feelings and emotions.

If you've built up the required trust, transparency, and reciprocity on your process, there is an opportunity to help the buyer reduce their homework. I highly recommend creating a list of RFP questions the client can include in their process. If they're "feeling" you, they'll include them in their process.

- You've saved the buyer time, as they will have less homework to do because you have already done it for them.
- You've saved yourself and your organization time: If the buyer uses *your* questions in their RFP, you've saved a lot of time because your answers are likely already ready. If the buyer does not use your questions, it is potentially an indicator that you are losing to a competitor.

While organizations have driven incredible amounts of rigor and process in their high consideration purchases, don't be fooled into believing that the end decision will still be made purely on logic. You can still influence decision processes through the continuation of building trust through every interaction, by creating value in every interaction, and by making things easy on the buyer in every interaction. Don't drive them to require more homework. Do the work for them, whether it's in providing RFP questions to ask, or simply through making the answers easy to understand and transparent.

...YOUR CONFERENCE BOOTH

Each year, our company attends a number of industry conferences. At each conference, we invest in the booth, the giveaway schwag, and the travel and associated expenses for a number of our sales team members.

At one retail conference, I saw a contact walking the floor who I recognized as an executive from Walmart. Walmart was one of the top five companies every vendor at the conference wanted as a client. The funny thing was, as I approached her, I noticed that the company name on her name tag was something different. She had signed up for the conference under a made-up company name to avoid being overwhelmed by sales pitches.

If that's the case, and attendees try their hardest to avoid getting sucked in to a booth, how do we more effectively woo attendees to engage us? What can we do differently from everyone else, while maximizing our investment in the show?

I discussed this phenomenon with a CEO I was networking with, Mark Attila Opauszky of PathFactory in Toronto. He explained that the key to disarming the brain's resistance to influence and attracting people to their booth was to not arm the booth with any salespeople at all. Instead, he armed the booth with customers, who wore shirts with labels identifying themselves as real customers instead of employees. While every booth in the vicinity was slow with traffic, his booth was packed and lead generation was more successful than they could have imagined.

Why did that work? Because conference attendees were interested in no-spin learning. It's interesting, unique, and an opportunity to network with their peers...in their booth!

How can you make your booth a magnet for your targets at conferences?

Consider the brain's resistance to influence, and how armed that resistance is for a potential prospect attending a conference. Potential influence is all around them. If having your customers attend on your behalf is unrealistic, arm your booth with your top client success representatives, solution consultants, or even your product team members. Then, make sure it's clear to any conference attendees who are walking the floor that your booth is a sales-free zone, and the attendees are not there to sell. T-shirts are cheap ways to do this, and so is posting signage in your booth indicating that your booth is a sales-free zone. Plus, your client success team, your solutions consultants, and your product team members will get invaluable feedback from prospective and current customers that they can take back to the rest of the organization.

Your non-sales approach and attendance at conferences will ironically result in more genuine interactions, trust building, and differentiation. It's not to say that your sales team members shouldn't attend conferences. However, to get a bigger bang in terms of lead generation, take conferences as an opportunity to differentiate your approach and attract more prospects.

Can you subsidize your customers' attendance in exchange for having them arm the booth? Can you send your client success team to arm the booth, or perhaps your product development team? Then, make it clear who they are, and you'll find your booth to be a magnet of quality conversation.

TRANSPARENCY AS A SALES CULTURE

Now, more than ever, being transparent to the outside world requires that you practice transparency inside your organization every single day. Would you be proud of the conversations and behaviors that take place within your organization? How about on your sales forecast calls? Would your forecast calls scare the bejeezus out of a potential buyer?

Here are the two biggest mistakes I see organizations make in their forecasts:

1. "What is your commit?": In one organization, sales reps were often asked to state their quarter forecast commitment in meetings. Sales reps in the room would often (a) fluff up their "commitment" numbers if they were coming in low, (b) fluff up their "commitment" numbers to get short-term blasts of dopamine associated with sounding impressive to their boss and peers, or (c) temper expectations by providing a lower number if they were on track to have a big quarter. The result of this approach is a consistently inaccurate forecast and a room full of uncomfortable salespeople.

2. Loss review calls: Opportunities will be lost, and in these cases, sales leaders are often heard attempting to cast blame, looking to point out every mistake the salesperson took through the buyer's journey. As a result, salespeople end up (a) hiding their losses from their peers, moving the close date out on a deal to avoid marking it as Closed-Lost in their CRM system, or (b) explaining the loss to their peers in a way that shifts the blame to others or unavoidable forces.

Foster a culture of transparency, where you are consistently celebrating accuracy versus chest puffing, and celebrating effort and learning over having a "losses are for losers" mentality.

During forecast reviews, encourage your teams to work together to create a forecast, then reward their accuracy. At PowerReviews, while we were learning how buyers buy, every month was another team forecast accuracy contest. Over time, from the learnings of these contests and the alignment of our sales process to our ability to recognize where the buyer was in their why change/ why us/why now journey, we were able to provide a ninety-day forecast that was consistently within 3% of our actual results.

If you're not losing, you're not trying. Nobody has a 100% win rate. Create a culture where losing is celebrated as opportunities to learn, where reps following a loss are recognized for their effort, and are encouraged to share what really happened. As a sales leader, remember the fact that your salesperson is already feeling the pain associated with a loss. The salesperson has invested time and effort, and the result from their effort is a big, fat zero.

Ask questions like, "What can you learn from this loss?" Or, "What will you do differently?" Even better, you might ask, "What can everyone learn from this loss?" Foster a culture of transparency. We are not perfect, so we will lose deals. Look to the winning competitor for lessons: How did they do it? What was it about their solution that led to their victory? Did the competition make them feel more certain in the expected result? Did the competition provide a pricing model that gave the buyer a better feeling of fairness? Does the competitive solution have the buying organization feeling as though they'll have more autonomy?

If you're in an environment where public commits and public shaming is an everyday occurrence, it may be time to find another home. The best leaders are fostering cultures of transparency and celebrating losses as opportunities to learn, develop, and improve.

AFTERWORD

THE END OF LYING?

T WAS AUGUST OF 2015. MY WIFE AND OUR THREE CHILDREN WERE heading out to California for a Disneyland vacation. In preparation for that trip, we boarded our three dogs at a local pet hotel in Palatine, Illinois, a suburb of Chicago.

Our children's anticipation of Disneyland was overflowing as we walked through the promenade outside on our way towards the entrance. The kids sang "Let it Go!" from the Disney movie *Frozen,* which was blasting through the promenade speakers. While it was really warm in Anaheim, our kids were prepared with their propeller misters, ready to dig in.

Just then, the phone rang. It was the owner of the boarding facility. They had lost one of our family members, our boy Digger, a forty-five-pound German Shepherd mix and rescue from a local foundation. Soft, gentle, and sweet. We often joked in the presence of our other dogs that Digger was our favorite.

As we stood in the mall area outside of Disneyland, the owner of the boarding facility explained that Digger had become agitated, bit a handler, then turned and scaled the eight-foot fence protecting the yard. He then went on to explain how, upon landing safely on the other side, he took off, and they had not been able to catch him.

Digger, the calmest and sweetest of our dogs, was always the one watching over our kids. He never did as much as put his paws up on our dog-run fence and had never even attempted to jump on our couch at home. We were flabbergasted at the thought of him acting out in this way and torn apart by the thought of him wandering the streets, running through traffic, likely searching for us, trying to find his way home.

That was only the beginning of the story. We were 2,000 miles away, entering "The Happiest Place on Earth" for the first time with our young children. My kids were crying their eyes out. After calling friends and neighbors soliciting their help, we entered Disneyland anyway. The substantial investment in tickets for the park had been made. We figured we could only control so much from so far away, so my wife and I made the decision to make the most of our plight.

While there were a number of unconfirmed sightings of Digger during the day, he was still lost. We were not enjoying ourselves, knowing that a family member was in turmoil, so we left the park and went back to the hotel. During a check-in conversation I had a few hours in to their search, the facility told us they were "taking a break" from looking, because Digger "was probably hiding somewhere." We couldn't sit still.

I started the process of building a marketing campaign to get the word out. I left a message on every lost dog website, posting on every social media channel, called everyone we knew, every shelter in the area, and every police station in the area to let them know we were looking for him, and handled inbound calls from people with tips and sightings.

Very quickly, everyone knew about Digger.

Over the next few weeks, media coverage started to grow. We were featured on Chicago's WGN-TV news when we arrived back home.

Then, the boarding facility started to push back. They were upset we had built up the media coverage, perceiving that it was causing undue attention on the fact that *they* lost him. After all, they had positioned it to us that it was Digger's fault. According to them, he acted out. He became a ninja and scaled a fence. He bit. They were now unwilling to participate in the story.

A local newspaper did manage to get an interview with one of the owners. The writer asked for the details, confused regarding the boarding facility's account of the story. How could a forty-five-pound dog climb an eight-foot fence with such speed, and also land well enough on the other side to speed off without injury? The co-owner of the facility replied that no one actually witnessed the occurrence, but went on to explain that the only way he could have gotten out was via the eight-foot fence.[1] This conversation between the facility owner and the journalist was the first of many inconsistencies in their story, which was the basis for our search.

Trust was gone. And, the Facebook community for Digger we had established to support the search exploded with growth, with well over 4,000 followers. Everyone within miles of our home now knew that the boarding facility had lost Digger and had bent the truth regarding what had happened.

Over time, their story changed a third time, to now include an explanation that he climbed a shorter fence, and placed blame on the garbage company who they claimed did not follow the proper protocol when picking up the garbage the day of disappearance. The third story was the best of the bunch, and if they had led with it, been transparent, owned the issue and told the truth, their business and relationship with the community would be considerably better. People make mistakes. Companies make mistakes. Own them.

During the following weeks, we continued to post signs in the community keeping Digger's disappearance top of mind. Digger is family to us, and we could

---

1   Peterson, Eric. "Did Digger the Dog Climb out of Facility?" Daily Herald, 17 Aug. 2015, www.dailyherald.com/article/20150814/news/150819350/

not stop looking. On the signs, in small font it identified that he had last been seen at the boarding facility. Pet search experts recommended that we put that fact on the signs, as (a) dogs are typically found within a small area surrounding where they were lost, and (b) some who find what they think are "stray" dogs often feel that the owner was negligent in letting them go, and therefore will just keep the dog. Especially a beauty like Digger.

These signs were of a high-quality material, weather and wind-proof, bright yellow with strong stakes for placing in the ground. One-by-one they disappeared. Often in the middle of the night.

What did we do? Well, we went big…and put up billboards. We posted on Facebook "try to steal this sign," a post that reached well over 200,000 viewers.

With the use of trail cameras and a huge following of individuals keeping an eye out, we caught the boarding facility taking the signs. They didn't admit to it until we had the proof. As a matter of fact, at one point in the process, their still loyal customers exclaimed, "They are not stealing your signs." Turns out they were. And after getting the police involved, they explained to the police that they wanted the signs down, because their business name was on them.

This is an extreme example of business deceit, eroding trust, and practicing the opposite of transparency. As of the time of this writing, it's been over three years and Digger is still missing. While our hearts will always hurt because our boy Digger has yet to be found, our lives were turned upside down because of the behaviors of this business. The lack of transparency resulted in a family in turmoil, but their business has suffered mightily as well.

In your business, you will make mistakes. You will have upset customers.

Hiding lies or spinning mistakes in business is a no-win proposition in today's digital age. I know it's pretty provocative to say that lying may be dying, as it would be the same to say that crime would disappear, which it won't. It has always been easier for an individual to manipulate someone through mistruth than holding them at gunpoint. The concept of #FakeNews is drawing a great deal of attention to mistruths in the media. Being able to decipher truth from lies is under siege.

Either way, putting customers first, applying your new found understanding of their brain function as it relates to decision making, and leveraging the concepts of unexpected honesty and transparency will become not only the norm, but the *minimum* acceptable criteria. Lead with it, control your sales cycles, build trust, accelerate decisions, make life a lot harder on your competitors, and win more often. The result will be more leads, higher lifetime value of your accounts, and many more referrals. Enjoy...#FindDigger.

ACKNOWLEDGMENTS

HOW DID THIS HAPPEN? ONE MOMENT I'M WORKING AS THE CHIEF revenue officer of a growing technology firm, and the next, I'm in a Starbucks for hours per day unloading my brain, in a library reading and researching, and in meetings asking a lot of questions about the book-writing journey. What you're holding wouldn't exist without the help of many, many others, and I'm weeping just writing this.

Let's start from the beginning:

I'm in New York one day, and pop in to see my friend and former co-worker, Jeff Rohrs. He introduces me to his CEO, telling that CEO that I'm known as an expert in *The Challenger Sale*. Ironically, I tell Jeff about my theories on transparency. He springs into action, hands me a book called *Non-Obvious* by Rohit Bhargava, and walks me through different paths to writing and publishing the book. He had me buying URLs by the end of the day, and really kick-started the process for me.

Then, there's Kyle Lacy and Liz Cain, who let me write an article for OpenView Venture Partners to help validate interest in the topic. Good news was, it certainly was validated by their audience.

Then, through Rohrs' encouragement, I connected with Rohit and his organization Ideapress Publishing. Rohit has been the guide to the day-to-day, along with Marnie McMahon. I appreciate that guidance, as well as their excitement for the topic, creativity around some of the elements, and confidence in me that I could put a whole pile of coherent sentences together. They provided a team to help me with this journey, including my editor Gretchen Gardner, who opened my eyes to what a great, valuable book this could be.

Next there's Scott Anschuetz, for being such a sounding board, supporter, encourager, and friend. The guy has a million things going on, but one Friday morning per month, every month, I can count on the fact that we will be on the phone at 8 a.m., and I'm prepped to have the heck mentored out of me. Scott, you don't realize how much you helped. And, the little things, like putting me in touch with brilliant minds, like Ben Kiker and Bud Michael, who helped me get rolling with some of the tactics, but also with the confidence that this would actually work.

And, of course, the new king of Chicago tech, Jeff Rosset, who has made so many connections for me, trusted me to execute really important events in his companies Sales Assembly (as a closing keynote speaker) and VentureSCALE (as the opening half-day trainer in his first cohort). Thanks, buddy!

Then there is Matt Moog, the CEO of PowerReviews and the guy who probably wanted to throw me down the stairs when I told him I was going to go on this journey, but who has been a supporter, encourager, and enabler for this journey.

Then there are people like Ethan Zoubek, who is such a no b.s. friend, who consistently helped me see the light on this project, and how to get there, all the way down to the technology I used to manage the writing process. And there were so many others who played roles in the execution, coordination, or encouragement category like Bryan Naas, Tom Corey at CoCreateFilms, Theresa O'Neil, Kira Meinzer, Michael Wyman (who taught me how to say no), John Philippo, and Jack Kusner.

I also want to thank Daniel Clark, lecturer at DePaul University, and expert in Behavioral Economics. He validated concepts here in this book that I thought had a decent chance at turning out to be complete and utter nonsense. Thanks for lying to me and telling me I'm on to something here!

I have to give a tear-jerking thanks to my friend Pete Lipovsek. I may have talked myself out of taking this journey multiple times if it wasn't for you, Pete. I will forever be grateful for you pushing me and helping me see how important it is to follow your passions, and not wait for the whole world to align around you. You told me to go make it happen, then told me again, then told me again. You are the best, brother!

To my family: First, my late mother-in-law, Sandy, who was my biggest fan in this process. When she passed, at her funeral, her friends (most of which I had never met) all came up to me and asked me about the book. She helped me see the stars align around pursuing this book and doing it now.

To my kids, including my step-daughter, Skye, who has such a passion for writing, but assured me that the topic of this book sounded "boring" and that she would likely never read it. My daughter, Eden, and my son, Luke, are the light in my life and keep me grounded around what truly matters.

To my parents, and specifically my Dad, who's in his mid-nineties and can't believe I left my job to write, but is the source of my personality, my sales foundation, my no-nerves-while-presenting-to-large-audiences DNA, and who gave me the best advice I've ever received: "In everything you do for an audience, like giving a speech, teaching a class, writing, etc., a percentage of that audience won't love it. Count on it. Every time. Take their feedback and learn from it but know they may never love it. You can't worry about those people. Cherish the ones who do, and focus on making their experience better, and better, and better."

And finally, to my wife, Christy, for being so incredible through this journey. You knew from the day you met me that I wanted to do this, and when I told you the time had come for me to go for it, and we would be shutting off our income for a while, there wasn't a single ounce of pushback...nothing but support, nothing but love, nothing but assurance that He will guide the way. Thank you! Along with the kids, you are really why I do much of anything.

For all of you reading, I hope you love the book, and if you don't, that's ok, too. Thanks, Dad, for helping me see that I should embrace being a 4.2-4.5. Let's see if we can pack this book full of reviews, and they average out to a solid 4.5! Seriously...go write a review :)

Online: www.transparencysale.com
Twitter: @tcaponi @TransprncySale
Facebook: @SalesMelon

READING LIST

As a sales historian, having read literally hundreds of books on sales, I came to the realization that in order to write something truly valuable, I needed to bring the voice of those who are outside of the sales world to the future of our profession. I purposely stayed away from re-reading old sales classics or picking up new ones. My focus was to explore the specifics regarding the fields of neuroscience (the study of the brain) as it relates to decision making, and neuromarketing (using neuroscience to optimize marketing and branding efforts). Here's the list that drove many of the thoughts and ideas scattered throughout the book:

Authenticity - Gilmore & Pine

Descartes' Error and *The Strange Order of Things* - Damasio

Buyology - Lindstrom

Into the Magic Shop - Doty

I Feel You - Beam

The YES Brain - Siegel & Bryson

Absolute Value - Simonson & Rosen

Supreme Influence - Niurka

Activate Your Brain - Halford

Who's in Charge? - Gazzaniga

The Man Who Mistook His Wife For A Hat - Sacks

The Knowledge Illusion - Sloman & Fernbach

The Buying Brain - Pradeep

Extreme Trust - Peppers & Rogers

Brainfluence - Dooley

A Field Guide to Lies - Levitin

Pre-Suasion - Cialdini

Tell the Truth - Unerman & Baskin

Quirk - Holmes

Annoying - Palca & Lichtman

AUTHOR BIO

An award-winning sales leader, Todd Caponi's passion is for all things sales methodology, learning theory, and decision science. His expertise is in building the revenue capacity for technology companies, having served in senior leadership roles, helping one organization to a successful IPO followed by an exit valued at almost $3B. He is a winner of an American Business "Stevie" Award for VP of WW Sales of the Year, and is also a former owner/operator of a sales training and consulting company.

INDEX

TOYS "R" US, 85, 86